SAMUEL BUTLER
(1835–1902)

SAMUEL BUTLER
(1835–1902)

by

P. N. FURBANK

CAMBRIDGE

at the University Press

1948

*Printed in Great Britain at the University Press, Cambridge
(Brooke Crutchley, University Printer)
and published by the Cambridge University Press
(Cambridge, and Bentley House, London)*

Agents for U.S.A., Canada, and India: Macmillan

CONTENTS

CONTENTS

FOREWORD

The ensuing study is presented in substantially the same form as that in which it was submitted for the Le Bas Prize. One chapter has, however, been omitted, on the advice of Professor Willey, to whose suggestions I am also indebted for a number of corrections of expression and the revision of one argument.

P. N. F.

BIBLIOGRAPHICAL NOTE

The editions of works by or about Butler in respect of which page-references are quoted are listed hereunder. Abbreviations employed are shown against titles to which they refer.

A. & S.	*Alps and Sanctuaries.* David Bogue, 1882.
EN.	*Erewhon.* Trubner, 1872.
E.O. & N.	*Evolution Old and New.* David Bogue, 1882.
E.R.	*Erewhon Revisited.* Grant Richards, 1901.
F.H.	*The Fair Haven.* Ed. Streatfeild. Cape, 1913.
F.Y.	*A First Year in Canterbury Settlement.* Longman, 1863.
L. & H.	*Life and Habit.* Trubner, 1878.
L. or C.	*Luck or Cunning?* A. C. Fifield, 1887.
NB.	*The Notebooks of Samuel Butler.* Ed. H. F. Jones. A. C. Fifield, 1912.
U.M.	*Unconscious Memory.* Ed. Hartog. A. C. Fifield, 1910.
W.O.A.F.	*The Way of All Flesh.* Grant Richards, 1903.
	After Puritanism. By HUGH KINGSMILL. Duckworth, 1929.
F.E.	*Further Extracts from the Notebooks of Samuel Butler.* Ed. A. T. Bartholomew. Cape, 1934.
F.J.	*Samuel Butler, a Memoir.* By H. F. JONES. Macmillan, 1919.
F.R.	*Samuel Butler and his Family Relations.* By Mrs R. S. GARNETT. Dent, 1926.

CHAPTER I

Butler and Muggeridge

THERE can be little doubt that Festing Jones's *Life of Butler* has done its subject a disservice. Butler was pre-eminently a man to have lived in his own books and in other people's anecdotes. It has been the experience of everyone reading the *Life* to feel that within its accumulation of detail Butler shrinks, and is almost explained away. And at such a dangerous point in the history of his reputation, when the scrupulousness of uncritical friendship had exhibited him so naked to the public gaze, it was inevitable that someone or other would soon take advantage of his unprotected state to handle him roughly. Desmond MacCarthy was kind, and supported the legend, while making fun of the details. Hugh Kingsmill in *After Puritanism* was less indulgent, and got so far as pointing out the hole in the defences, though not ready himself to make the attack. With Malcolm Muggeridge's *The Earnest Atheist*, in 1936, came the full onslaught. Poor Butler! The very lateness of the attack made it the more devastating. In Malcolm Muggeridge there was all the cleverness and the taste for prey to make things uncomfortable for a figure much less unprotected than Butler. Even more striking is the suitability of the moment. For this was the moment of beginning nostalgia for the Victorian period and of revulsion against other anti-Victorians than Butler. The inevitable boyhood enthusiasm for Shaw, for Wilde, and for Ibsen, and the recovery from it, was having a permanent effect on their reputations. On the other hand, this was the moment for biographies of the Sad Young Man. The years just preceding the second world war made quite a distinct genre of these;

accounts tumbled from the press, each more scarifying than the preceding, of the unhappy childhood, of pathological disasters in adolescence, and so on. In Butler there was a perfect victim and Muggeridge's book conveys a sense of vicarious masochism quite in keeping with this very type of autobiography. As in the strict example of the type, we read on with a growing and eager horror as new degradations are heaped upon the Sad Young Man's head. There is a mounting glee, an intoxication, in the harrying of the subject that is far more characteristic of autobiography than of biography. Whether this was opportunism on the part of its writer, or simply the consequence of the coincidence of a desire to write a novel that was in this fashion with so admirable a chance to do it vicariously and with no expense to its author, I feel uncertain. But the result was the same. We were ready for a novel of this type, and we had the less defence against it in that it turned up in the guise of a critical biography. Further, there was the prestige of our new return to Duty, our revulsion against anti-Victorianism. The coincidence of two such attitudes could not help but produce something fairly convincing, and convincing *The Earnest Atheist* was. My object in this chapter will necessarily be to discredit, at least in part, the portrait contained in Muggeridge's book. But I am forced to admit that, irritating and bad in taste as Muggeridge's attack upon Butler is, my difficulty is not merely that of disentangling the specific criticism of Butler from what in this book appears to me as the extraneous novel-writing element in it, or from what I think to have a force borrowed from a lucky coincidence of two temporary attitudes of the public at the time of its writing, attitudes for the indulgence of which Butler was made unfairly a victim. For had the book not contained these extraneous elements, it would still have proposed some very necessary adjustments to our picture of Butler, and some less certainly necessary suggestions about the origin of the Butler legend which still offer considerable trouble to refute.

For if we discount the criticism to which Butler was exposed during his lifetime, against which he may safely be left to defend himself without coming off too badly, opinion of him up to *The Earnest Atheist* fell into two schools, in neither of which can one feel happy. There was the school of the 'friends of Samuel Butler', the people who wrote prefaces to the Fifield edition of his books, Festing Jones himself, A. T. Bartholomew, Professor M. Hartog and so on. These were content to continue Butler's own method of defending himself, but had hardly the talent for doing so. Without necessarily accepting Muggeridge's whole case against Festing Jones, one cannot but feel a distaste for some of the activities in which he engaged in Butler's name after the latter's death. The Butler dinners we may excuse, though we may be repelled by their odour of club orthodoxy and club jokes, by the vulgarity of menus embossed with a quotation from *Life and Habit*, and are bound to feel the sense of disappointment at this sort of final *taming* of the once formidable outlaw. But there are other things less excusable; the tidying-up of Butler, noted by Muggeridge, the suppression of the more outspoken of the sonnets, the falsification of his dying words. It amounts to an attempt, not only to keep Butler's name alive until the publication of the *Life*, but to make him respectable, to make a sort of orthodoxy of Butlerism.

Professor Hartog's preface to the 1912 edition of *Unconscious Memory* is even more of a case in point. One could hardly wish for a better example of the vicious 'authoritative' approach against which this book is directed than this very preface, with its attempt to bestow orthodoxy upon Butler; Butler himself found no worse example of the debased scientific style, the language at once timid and pretentious, the compound of borrowed theory and borrowed jargon, inexhaustible of references and indefatigable in its effort to avoid what would commit its author.

On the other hand, we have the sympathetic but reasonably critical attitude, of which the best examples are to be found in scattered remarks by Desmond MacCarthy, in Hugh Kingsmill's essay in *After Puritanism*, and in that by Middleton Murry in *Aspects of Literature*. This leaves us quite as uneasy. In the space of a few pages and by casual admissions only, these three writers suggest degrees of folly or inadequacy in Butler, and discrepancies between the popular reputation and the fact, that seem pretty well irreconcilable with the kind of respect with which they regard him. You feel that they should have said either less or more; that they themselves have not realized, or do not care to admit, the extent of the objections that they have suggested. Most of Muggeridge's case indeed is to be found in critics quite favourable to Butler, his chief addition to it resting simply in his special degree of animosity.

Middleton Murry, for instance, remarks very justly that whereas before reading the *Life*, one could think of Butler's theory of the feminine authorship of the *Odyssey* as an amusing freak with no great bearing upon his serious reputation, one is forced, upon learning that he spent ten years' more or less uninterrupted work upon it, to think of the matter, and therefore of Butler, rather differently. And certainly, for any one who takes Butler at all seriously, this does not overstate the case. If you are unwilling to accept Muggeridge's explanation of the facts, you are more or less bound to provide a different one. Particularly is this so, in that the accepted picture of Butler is very much that of a man whose *whole* attitude matters. In this picture, he is one of the late-Victorian 'prophets', one of the people demanding submission to their whole system, and in whose life the discovery of such a considerable misdirection is liable to discredit their whole programme of living.

By omission, therefore, Middleton Murry and similar critics left it as their obvious opinion that Butler could not, at least, sustain any longer a reputation as a 'prophet'. But by their failure to show in any adequate manner where they did look in Butler for the kind of value that they apparently attributed to him, and how one should reconcile to oneself the lapses and the waste-products in Butler with what was valuable in him, they left him exposed to an attack which was as much an *overall* attack as the picture of Butler as the prophet was an overall glorification.

The position is, therefore, that the last word upon Butler is at present a wholesale slaughter of his reputation as a character and writer, and that the only sympathetic yet intelligent criticism of him before the date of this total attack is of a kind that rather opens the way for such an attack than defends him from it.

The form of Muggeridge's case against Butler is, in its simplest terms, this: 'Butler exhibits a sick and unsuccessful personality' (here follows the novel-writing element to which I have referred, the portrait of the conventional Sad Young Man), 'hence he could not have written anything of real value to us in ordering our own lives, hence the secret of his reputation must lie in extraneous causes, viz. that he said something that people wanted and were waiting to hear.' Clearly, then, to oppose this case, the only fair course is to dispute the version of Butler's personality.

The case against *The Earnest Atheist* may be fairly bluntly stated. It is briefly this: whereas it seems fairly evident that a combat more or less of the kind described by Muggeridge did take place in Butler's spirit, yet Muggeridge goes wrong when he infers that Butler came off from this combat unsuccessfully. What leads me to think this, is the one obvious flaw in Muggeridge's book, the awkwardness of its few references to Butler's talent. If Muggeridge had been content merely to diagnose Butler as a sick soul and left it at that, his position would have been sounder. As it is, he has several unobtrusive and more or less uncritical references to Butler's 'skill in writing', his 'ability as a satirist' and so on; and these references raise obvious questions about the relation of a writer's spiritual maladies to the intrinsic value of his work. These are questions which might have been avoided easily enough, and the fact that they were not avoided is evidence of a certain uneasiness on Muggeridge's part. Talent in the sort of writing engaged upon by Butler is clearly not merely equivalent to 'skill' in any restricted sense. And the kind of power exhibited in *Erewhon* is something that prompts us to look for its roots fairly deep into the writer's nature. Yet if we are to do that, we are led to see the enormous difficulty of believing that a writer who could make such extraordinary artistic use of his own experience was still incapable of making any valuable personal use of it; that, in fact, his personal resistance to his own temperamental misfortunes had been merely feeble and indeed quite pathologically weak. In suggesting that Butler did not show any worth-while talent, and that the source of his reputation is to be found in the lucky hitting-off of a fashion in feeling in the public, Muggeridge would have had at least a self-consistent case. But by his admission of talent of a certain value, he succeeds in drawing attention to the inadequacy of his own admission; and one begins to see that this inadequacy is a necessary consequence of the kind of treatment given to Butler's personal problem.

For what it is necessary to observe before any other quality in Butler's work is a savage strength, a strength quite out of keeping with the pervading weakness of the picture of Butler in *The Earnest Atheist*. Swift is the classical English satirist, his is the norm and model of all satire, and the obvious method of praising any subsequent satirist is to liken him to Swift. Yet if we take another Utopian satirist; if we take, for instance, Morris and his *News from Nowhere*, what most enforces the contrast of this placid, bloodless, bluestocking piece of ingenuity, is surely the absence in it, as compared with Butler, of the quality of savagery. Let it be asserted at once that no serious effort should or can be made to sustain Butler as a rival of Swift. There is here all the difference between a major and a minor writer. None the less, I should suggest that where we are most conscious of the strength of Butler, at least in *Erewhon*, is in those places where more than a trace of the same controlled savage power is exhibited. *Erewhon* is a comparatively good-humoured book, and it is a book whose excellencies are not all of one kind. Yet we may say that the part of it which most immediately catches the imagination, the part which it is most difficult to dismiss from the mind, and which we tend to think of as most essentially constituting the book, is that which deals with the Erewhonian attitude to crime and disease, and the trials of offenders against the laws of health.

Prisoner at the bar, you have been accused of the great crime of labouring under pulmonary consumption, and after an impartial trial before a jury of your countrymen, you have been found guilty. Against

7

the justice of the verdict I can say nothing; the evidence against you was conclusive, and it only remains for me to pass such a sentence upon you as shall satisfy the ends of the law. That sentence must be a very severe one. It pains me much to see one who is yet so young, and whose prospects in life were otherwise so excellent, brought to this distressing condition by a constitution which I can only regard as radically vicious; but yours is no case for compassion; this is not your first offence; you have led a career of crime, and have only profited by the leniency shown you upon past occasions to offend yet more seriously against the laws and institutions of your country. You were convicted of aggravated bronchitis last year; and I find that, though you are now only twenty-three years old, you have been imprisoned on no less than fourteen occasions for illnesses of a more or less hateful character; in fact, it is not too much to say that you have spent the greater part of your life in a jail. (*EN.* 96)

The reaction to this is of the same kind as the reaction to Swift's *Modest Proposal*. We cannot persuade ourselves that it is merely the formal trick of irony that gives the peculiar unsettling force to this passage. Its effect upon us is something that will not easily be explained away. It hits the reader at a hidden but specially vulnerable point. When we have stated to ourselves the bearing of it, the way in which it deflects our natural feelings of indignation against the patent injustices of an obviously unnatural system, upon the less obvious injustices of the traditional legal system, we are left with a balance of animus that has still to be accounted for. The passage sets up a condition of anxiety in the reader before he has formed any clear notion of the reform that it is its immediate object to recommend, and this anxiety persists after the merit of the recommendation has been considered and decided upon. The anxiety, in fact, goes deeper than the indignation which it is called upon to stimulate. It is a species of personal disquietude that no amount of good resolution in regard to the treatment of criminals can fully allay. In this it has a parallel in the

8

Modest Proposal. The element of insoluble dilemma in the offered situation provokes a reaction of a more personal kind than satire can as a rule attain.

I suggest that here we have a clue to Butler's own personal situation that is worth considering. Butler being so persistent a worrier of ideas (to the extent that there is hardly a leading notion of his that at one time or another, in his published works or his Notebooks, we do not feel that he has run a trifle too often or too hard) it is unlikely that, if the real attraction for him of his paradoxes upon the relations of crime and disease had been the assistance they lent to the doctrine of the remedial treatment of criminals, we should not have found these views elaborated, and repeated in forms other than satiric, in numerous other passages and books. Since they are not repeated, the suggestion is that the force that we feel behind this ironic situation is something generated in Butler's struggle with his own more intimate dilemma. For in Butler's life we must see not, as Muggeridge would have it, a prolonged, unsuccessful, nagging quarrel between two halves of a discordant nature, but a violent, devastating and comparatively short battle in early manhood, from which he emerged in some ways immensely strengthened, though in others irretrievably scarred, crippled and benumbed.

The falsification that results from the conventionality and vulgarity of Muggeridge's portrait of Butler seems here to be indicated. It lies in the failure to see that what distinguishes the course taken in Butler by that combat between discordant selves with which we are familiar is the violent, almost heroic, self-preservative force which it brought out in him. One need go no further than the pages of William James's *Varieties of Religious Experience* to satisfy oneself that the sort of calamity that befell Butler was not of itself

common one. It shows, therefore, a certain blameable
—ty of approach to the matter, to insist upon the com-
—place symptoms of such a disorder, whilst overlooking
what most calls for a special attention, that is, the peculiar
nature of the subject's resistance to it. For to quite a considerable extent what we think of as the talent or the genius
of Butler is the outward evidence of the special power that
he derived from that life-and-death struggle which seems
to have taken place in his own nature as a young man.

The Way of all Flesh belongs essentially to the literature
of Conversion. And to look at it in this light is a good way
of fixing to oneself its distinctively modern position. When
we examine those painful recognitions and reversals of
feeling which the book records, we see at once that they
have a characteristic which separates them fundamentally
from the moments of conversion in Christian autobiography.
The incident of the meeting of Ernest Pontifex with
Towneley in a street near Ashpit Place is a case in point.

> Towneley said a few words of common form to Ernest about his
> profession as being what he thought would be most likely to interest
> him, and Ernest, still confused and shy, gave him for lack of some-
> thing better to say his little threepenny-bit about poor people being
> so very nice. Towneley took this for what it was worth and nodded
> assent, whereupon Ernest imprudently went further and said, 'Don't
> you like poor people very much yourself?'
>
> Towneley gave his face a comical but good-natured screw, and
> said quietly, but slowly and decidedly, 'No, no, no,' and escaped.
>
> (*W.O.A.F.* 261)

There is a recognizable affinity between this and incidents
in the histories of Christian conversion. A certain historical
interest, therefore, seems to attach to the nature of the
obvious difference between them. For the weight behind
this experience of Ernest's is not only that of the won-
dering 'How did I become this?—how did I become a

creature capable of making this remark?', it is ⸻
recognizing that the forces that have brought th⸻
this point are too strong to lose their hold mere⸻
recognized for what they are. The pain is not m⸻
contrast between the two ways of life, but in th⸻
of the impossibility *by now* of any complete conversion from
the one to the other. The shock of the confrontation and
the recognition of a different way of life is so sharp because
of the actual ignorance of Ernest of the possibilities represented by Towneley. The whole weight of the book is
behind the demonstration that given a certain background
and a certain heredity, the victim of these chooses nothing
at all for himself, and is in fact not given an opportunity of
choice. With Bunyan and with St Augustine, much is known
about the other way of life before the conversion is made;
it is, in fact, a conversion from the known to the known.
With the kind of experience dealt with in *The Way of All
Flesh*, the conversion, or the desire for conversion, is
between the known and the unknown. There is a total dis-
continuity between the values of the Ernest of the Ashpit-
Place ministry and those of Towneley (Towneley, indeed,
never being seen in the book from any other standpoint
than Ernest's immediate view of him from across the gulf
of their impassable difference). It is not a matter of the
opposition of what they severally represent, but of the
entire alienness of the one to the other. Up to now there
has been no question of choice for Ernest; he is as it were
a collection of the threepenny-bits that other people have
bestowed upon him. And the necessity has become obviously
that of winning, at any expense, the right to choose. On
the other hand, it has become equally clear that though the
right to choose might easily be his, the power of choosing
certain alternatives was already gone. He would have to

ave been born again of different parents and indeed great-grand-parents to be in a position to break altogether out of the ring of his personality.

If we lay hold of the dilemma represented by the meeting of Ernest Pontifex with Towneley, we have a good entry into the whole matter of Butler and his writing. In addition to the relation of this dilemma to the very nature and internal character of Butler's talent and personality, it has the closest possible connection with other of his commonest expressed ideas.

We shall have these crude and subversionary books from time to time, until it is recognized as an axiom of morality that luck is the only fit object of human veneration.... (*F.E.* 20)

So Butler writes in his Notebook '...of some very respectable work on morality—the Bible for example'. Hardly a book of his but possesses in one or other form this notion of the virtue of being lucky. So, again, the note *Health before Honesty*:

It is not the interest of honesty or talent or virtue, but that of health and happiness that should take the highest place. Honesty is made for happiness, not happiness for honesty. (*F.E.* 23)

Or this from *Alps and Sanctuaries*:

The only thing that can produce a deep and permanently good influence upon a man's character is to have been begotten of good ancestors for many generations—or at any rate to have reverted to good ancestors—and to live among nice people. (*A. & S.* 327)

Or again from *The Way of All Flesh*:

Why cannot we be buried as eggs in neat little cells with ten or twenty thousand pounds each wrapped round us in Bank of England notes, and wake up as the sphex wasp does, to find that its papa and mamma have not only left ample provision at its elbow, but have been eaten by sparrows some weeks before it began to live consciously on its own account? (*W.O.A.F.* 81)

The virtue of luck, the morality of health, the duty to be born of good ancestry, the reverence due to money, all these notions, and numbers of others with which we grow familiar in the Notebooks and elsewhere, relate directly to the central dilemma that I refer to.

What I have said earlier of a passage from *Erewhon*, concerned with the relations of crime and disease, begins to fall into place. The force and depth of feeling conveyed by this passage has everything to do with the personal dilemma of Ernest Pontifex. Here, by the cruellest and most irresistible means, a legal trial, are enforced the laws which are represented in the dilemma. To be ill is a crime, because the true virtue is to be lucky—to be born healthy, or of the right ancestry, or with twenty thousand pounds wrapped round your egg, in the place of parents. Ernest Pontifex, indeed, had little more chance of being other than he was than the Erewhonian criminal had of avoiding consumption of the lungs.

If one wanted to enforce the supposition of the personal nature of the feeling behind this passage, there might be some interest in showing the frequency with which the idea of a *trial* occurs in mental struggle. An obvious piece of evidence would be found in Kafka. One might also recall the remark of Dr Johnson to the effect that the condition of a man who deliberately defends himself in his own mind against imaginary accusations in a court of law, is only distinguished by the degree of frequency of his indulgence in this, from the state of madness.

This, however, would be liable to mislead. It would be the greatest mistake to suggest that what lies behind the passage from *Erewhon* is the Ernest-Towneley experience as such. The last thing one wants to infer is that *Erewhon* depends for its enjoyment upon a knowledge of Butler's

13

own history. *Erewhon* is the most self-sufficient of Butler's books, and to my mind the most completely satisfactory one. It is to be regarded as the first-fruits of Butler's successful issue from that combat which was the central event of his life; and if one regards it as such, the roundness and the objectivity of the satire is to be seen as a sign of that very success. The savagery and fire of the early successful chapters of *The Way of All Flesh* are to be found equally in *Erewhon* and are the source of the power which it has to take hold of the imagination. But it is only because the personal experience involved has been successfully submerged and disengaged from its immediate personal associations that the writing can show such a power of good-humoured control.

My attempt in this study is to suggest a solution to the difficulty that is felt in reconciling the total rightness and strength of *Erewhon* with the weaknesses and false directions which Butler's talent sometimes takes elsewhere; and I want to do it by referring both to the peculiar nature of that experience which is recorded in *The Way of All Flesh*. But before saying more of that experience, it is worth insisting a little more on the need to treat Butler's writing on terms of the same kind, if not the same, as my own. I have spoken of a dilemma of which Butler was conscious, and of the overriding ideas of which it was the source. And whether or not that is the right way to think of that matter, the conclusion cannot be avoided that some mental factor must have existed in Butler which linked that knot of ideas which is to be seen constantly reforming, and appearing under different guises, throughout the writings on evolution and the travel-studies as much, almost, as in the Notebooks themselves. When one has got into the mood of Butler's Notebooks, one is aware of a break between notes that have a personal bearing—that seem to refer to a concealed *idée fixe*, of which the note is a tiny and partial rendering—and notes upon indifferent matters. There are comparatively few of the latter, and these when witty in form are quite dull, though when other than witty sometimes very charming (for instance, the delightful 'Eating Grapes Downwards'). The writings upon evolution leave one with a similar feeling. Disinterested play of the intelligence is in them so much overlaid by personal elements that the two can hardly be disentangled. The theory of the identity of heredity with unconscious memory merges imperceptibly into the picture of Butler's ideal man, the man to whom life comes easiest, the possessor of grace, the man for whom the greatest number of activities have reached the state of unconscious ease and perfection. The whole difference of the once-born and the twice-born is involved in the theory from the moment of its promulgation in *Life and Habit*. What gives the most lasting interest to the later books on evolution is perhaps the effort to bring to light the existence and the dangers of a new sort of orthodoxy, the scientific one. The attack upon this orthodoxy, and upon its chief representative in Darwin, is not distinguishable from the attack upon the Theobalds and Skinners. One of Butler's best strokes in the course of these attacks is to compare the tone of a particular kind of contemporary scientific writing with that of theological apologetics; so the connection from *The Way of All Flesh* via *The Fair Haven* to *Luck or Cunning?* is complete. The controversy with Darwin, whatever the rights and wrongs of the case, shows the personal element in Butler's attitude intruding injuriously. A nagging sense of a universal grievance is the stimulus of Butler's part in this matter; it is this which will not allow him to let it alone, and which makes him fanatical and sometimes tedious on the subject.

But the general assault upon Darwin and the new legend surrounding the scientist, which, for all its probable injustice to individuals, becomes so amusing and convincing in *Luck or Cunning?* is at once but another illustration of Butler's most deep-seated notions about life, and an inextricable part of the particular polemical case that he has in mind. So, too, the rehabilitation of the earlier writers upon evolution, of Buffon and Lamarck and Erasmus Darwin, takes on an immediate personal complexion. The inquiry into the history of the evolutionary theory no doubt began from the merest dispassionate curiosity, yet the personal application once made, the nature of the inquiry was irredeemably changed. The force of the writing is derived from this change, but the effect of the change is to take the writing out of the field of scientific controversy. One is no longer in the same world as that of the Darwinian writings. And this is not a simple matter of extraneous elements added to a piece of scientific polemic; the defence of the posthumous fame of Buffon and Erasmus Darwin comes to be the whole point of the case; it radically transforms the discussion and cannot subsequently be separated from the other elements in it. We have said that the inquiry no doubt began dispassionately and with no personal application in mind; and the same thing may be observed in the fate of details as of larger issues. A play of fancy in *Life and Habit*, upon the possibility of considering human beings as parasites upon a giant creature of another race, leads quite naturally into a tone of the strongest personal feeling:

a body. . . with organs, senses, dimensions in some way analogous to our own, into some other part of which being at the time of our great change we must infallibly re-enter, starting clean anew, with bygones bygone, and no more ache for ever from either age or antecedents.

(*L. & H.* 111)

The larger theme cannot be kept out. However distant a notion starts in this writing, it is attracted towards the emotional centre. The facts about the sphex wasp survive the books on evolution only to receive their personal application in *The Way of All Flesh*.

That in writings upon such diverse subjects as Butler's we should be constantly aware of the same tone of voice and the same small set of themes, suggests that the stimulus to writing must have been fairly intimate in nature. We cannot therefore get out of the necessity for examining the evidence as to Butler's personal experience. And as to what this experience was, I feel confident that Muggeridge's view can only mislead.

> I had to steal my own birthright. I stole it, and was bitterly punished. But I saved my soul alive. (*NB*. 182)

These sentences from the Notebooks seem to contain the whole matter. Butler's experience was of the nature of a violent and primitive effort for survival. When we think of the facts of Butler's childhood, as we know them, our natural reaction is to think of his version of them as an irritable exaggeration. Mrs Garnett, perhaps, can hardly convince us that his view of his own family was as far from the truth as she would have it believed. Theobald, Christina and Charlotte are unmistakably there in the occasional revealing admissions of her defence of their prototypes. None the less, the extraordinary brutality and reforming rage of the earlier chapters of *The Way of All Flesh* does seem at first sight considerably in excess of the given facts.

> 'I have sent him up to bed', said Theobald, as he returned to the drawing-room, 'and now, Christina, I think we will have the servants in to prayers', and he rang the bell for them, red-handed as he was. (*W.O.A.F.* 98)

Thus ends the incident of Ernest's beating for his slowness in learning to pronounce a certain letter of the alphabet. There is no doubt about the seriousness of the condemnation. 'Red-handed' is meant to bear its very fullest weight. The crime is one of blood, though perhaps no blood has been drawn. The offence is thought of as something mortal, as something to be connected with a primitive state of society, where father and son might be the most natural and the fiercest of enemies, ready to shed each other's blood. It is a joke when afterwards he talks thus of 'Near Relations':

> The Ancients attached such special horror to the murder of near relations because the temptation was felt on all hands to be so great that nothing short of this could stop people from laying violent hands upon them. The fable of the Erinyes was probably invented by fathers and mothers and uncles and aunts. (*F.E.* 91)

But the joke is very much like the truth. The preoccupation with the death of the father is not dictated merely by the sense of the convenience, under given circumstances, of being free from one's parents. There is the constant suggestion of a special virtue in the actual killing of the father, a suggestion that life is something to be stolen from the father by violence.

> Those who have never had a father can at any rate never know the sweets of losing one. To most men the death of his father is a new lease of life. (*F.E.* 90)

As a single casual note the effect of this is perhaps not felt as anything deadly: but with the weight of a hundred such remarks behind it, it takes a new and more literal import. 'I had to steal my birthright': this is the language of primitive law. It is clear that the rage which enflames the writer in *The Way of All Flesh* has been satisfied with

nothing less than the complete annihilation of the father—
or, which is the most of which society permits, of the
father's part in him. It is a modern version of slaying the
father and stealing his wives. The break with the 'Langar'
self took for Butler the colour of patricide.

Other things support this impression. The preoccupation
with the death of parents, which may be considered to have
a sort of virtue as a re-enactment of the 'murder' of the
father, is in a number of places connected with the theme
of money. Money is the most constantly recurring notion
in all Butler's writing. Wherever an image or an illustration is required, money is the idea readiest to hand. **NB**

Money, if it live at all, that is to say if it be reproductive and put
out at any interest, however low, is mortal and doomed to be lost
one day, though it may go on living through many generations of
one single family if it be taken care of. No man is absolutely safe.
It may be said to any man, 'Thou fool, this night thy money shall
be required of thee.' And reputation is like money: it may be
required of us without warning. The little unsuspected evil on which
we trip may swell up in a moment and prove to be the huge, Janus-
like mountain of unpardonable sin. And his health may be required
of any fool, any night or any day.

A man will feel loss of money more keenly than loss of bodily
health so long as he can keep his money. Take his money away and
deprive him of the means of earning any more, and his health will
soon break up; but leave him his money and, even though his health
breaks up and he dies, he does not mind it so much as we think.
Money losses are the worst, loss of health is next worst and loss of
reputation comes in a bad third. All other things are amusements
provided money, health and good name are untouched. (*NB*. 37) **NB**

This is but one example out of hundreds. The parody of
a theological style is entirely characteristic. There has been
a genuine transference of religious sentiment from its conventional objects to money. The eloquence convinces; the
temper of the writing has a sudden increase of warmth.

The language of Christian Stoicism comes very readily from Butler; substitute 'Honour' or 'Immortal soul' for 'Money' and the reality of the sentiment is undisguised. Any magnification of money becomes attractive to Butler. All the pet themes have at one time or another to be tried out upon money.

> If a man is to die rich, he must go through the embryonic stages with his money as much as with his limbs. *(F.E. 32)*

> Money is life, as it were capitalized. Life is that income derived from the capital investments of our forefathers. Money is to life much as matter to ether. *(F.E. 263)*

One cannot imagine the writings upon evolution without money as the perennial term of reference. Nor, again, could anything be more characteristic than this:

> When the snow bones lie it is said there will come more snow to bury them. And after a great money calamity, if the money bones lie, there will come more money. *(F.E. 110)*

Money is placed by this at the very centre of the sensible world; such intimate connotations has the word 'Money' for Butler, it is a natural twin of the word 'Bones'. All the evidence points to a superstitious feeling about money, and for this a reason may easily be suggested. Money is typical of the stolen birthright. It is something taken by force in the course of the imaginary patricide. And being taken by force, it comes to represent force in itself. It becomes a talisman as well as a trophy.

> Next to sexual matters there are none upon which there is such complete reserve between parents and children as on those connected with money. *(NB. 30)*

The connection with sexual matters is significant. The notion of the breaking into the guarded orchard, and the

20

carrying off of the prize, apply commonly to sexual matters, while here they are felt more strongly in regard to money.

This is not the only piece of evidence for our theory. Another characteristic of Butler's work, quite as fundamental, though more diffused and disguised and therefore less easy to pin down, points equally to our version of the facts. I mean by this Butler's peculiar reaction to the subject of Possession, to the significance, that is, of the words 'one's own'. A tiny fact observed in reading the Notebooks has its point here. Butler has written in 1883 a note on the relations between the Old Masters in painting and their pupils, in the course of which note he refers favourably to Titian. In 1897 this postscript is added:

I have changed my mind about Titian. I don't like him.

(*NB*. 135)

Now this note and its postscript were clearly not addressed to any one in particular. Had the question of publication been strongly in Butler's mind, he would naturally have tidied the whole note up. The recording of the simple fact that he had decided upon not liking Titian means plainly that the fact was thought to be important in itself. To have made up his mind upon the subject of a liking or its opposite had a special value for Butler. Everywhere the insistence is that one's opinion shall be one's own, and 'one's own' begins to take on the colour of a valuable possession, another kind of prize or trophy carried off from the world, or, in a different light, a protective good, something to fortify one against attacks or to preserve oneself against mere emptiness or destitution. Likes and dislikes are to be thought a kind of property. In the note 'On Knowing what gives us pleasure', a whole discipline is suggested for those who want to assure themselves of their own likes and dislikes.

To those, however, who are desirous of knowing what gives them pleasure but do not quite know how to set about it I have no better advice to give than that they must take the same pains about acquiring this difficult art as about any other, and must acquire it in the same way—that is by attending to one thing at a time and not being in too great a hurry. Proficiency is not to be attained here, any more than elsewhere, by short cuts or by getting other people to do work that no other than oneself can do. Above all things it is necessary here, as in all other branches of study, not to think we know a thing before we do know it—to make sure of our ground and be quite certain that we really do like a thing before we say we do. When you cannot decide whether you like a thing or not, nothing is easier than to say so and to hang it up among the uncertainties. Or when you know you do not know and are in such doubt as to see no chance of deciding, then you may take one side or the other provisionally and throw yourself into it. This will sometimes make you uncomfortable, and you will feel you have taken the wrong side and thus learn that the other was the right one. Sometimes you will feel you have done right. Any way ere long you will know more about it. But there must have been a secret treaty with yourself to the effect that the decision was provisional only. For, after all, the most important first principle in this matter is the not lightly thinking you know what you like till you have made sure of your ground. I was nearly forty before I felt how stupid it was to pretend to know things that I did not know and I still often catch myself doing so. Not one of my schoolmasters taught me this, but altogether otherwise.

(NB. 208)

To this we may add:

To know whether you are enjoying a piece of music or not you must see whether you find yourself looking at the advertisements of Pears' soap at the end of the programme. *(NB. 209)*

The inference all along is that likes are to be chosen upon the same plan as personal belongings. One is to apply to likes the same standards as are applied to possessions, to the extent even of insisting that they shall be one's own likes altogether and not merely in part—that, in fact, they are not ours at all until they are ours altogether. Hence

Butler's strangely proprietary attitude towards his own likes in art and elsewhere. We have Handel and Giovanni Bellini thrust down our throat so repeatedly, not because Butler could find nothing to enjoy or admire in other musicians or painters, but because he could not own the others totally as he could these. He understands and enjoys a good deal of Beethoven, but not all Beethoven. Beethoven, therefore, has to be given up. What is not Butler's own in Beethoven is somebody else's, and the 'somebody else' is bound to be an enemy. Butler cannot share his property in Beethoven with another, and therefore must abandon what he is holding. The alien portion of Beethoven cannot possibly be other than hostile to Butler's own portion, and must make it therefore not worth having. An account of a visit to a Philharmonic concert, recorded in the Note-books, has some interest here:

We went last night to the Philharmonic and sat in the shilling orchestra, just behind the drums, so that we could see and hear what each instrument was doing. (*NB.* 132)

This is not merely the provincial's desire to get his money's worth; it is a practical application of Butler's whole attitude to matters of taste; it represents the intention to sit in judgement, to bring the whole proceeding to trial, and to get the most favourable position for seeing that there is no deception. Butler goes to a concert in the sort of sceptical mood in which one might go to an evening of table-rapping.

The concert began with Mozart's G Minor Symphony. We liked this fairly well, especially the last Movement, but we found all the Movements too long and, speaking for myself, if I had a tame orchestra for which I might write programmes, I should probably put it down once or twice again, not from any spontaneous wish to hear more of it but as a matter of duty that I might judge it with fuller comprehension—still, if each movement had been half as long

I should probably have felt cordially enough towards it, except of course in so far as that the spirit of the music is alien to that of the early Italian school with which alone I am in genuine sympathy and of which Handel is the climax. (*NB.* 132)

In the end of this, we have a good practical example of the working of the property-interest in music. Butler has rights of ownership in the 'early Italian school . . . of which Handel is the climax', and it will therefore constitute *ipso facto* a more or less final objection to a musical style that it should not belong to this school. Something in the tone of the passage suggests that Mozart has been tested and has failed and retires from Butler's life quietly and for ever; Butler is, as it were, generous enough to wish he could give Mozart another chance or two, from the kind of responsibility that one feels towards any foreigner who is not an avowed enemy; but circumstances not allowing of this, Mozart must take the present dismissal as final.

Then came a terribly long-winded recitative by Beethoven and an air with a good deal of 'Che farò' in it. I do not mind this, and if it had been 'Che farò' absolutely I should, I daresay, have liked it better. I never want to hear it again and my orchestra should never play it. (*NB.* 132)

The assumption of *naïveté*, of directness of reaction, may be seen to be theoretical; the obtrusion of the question as to whether he would have this played upon his own orchestra is another application of the notion of ownership; it is the question whether one can adopt this, whether one can appropriate it to oneself. (What true *naïveté* in this situation will produce is something quite different. A pleasant example is to be seen in Parson Woodforde's Diary:

The Concert was very fine indeed, and Madame Mara, the famous Singer, sung delightfully. I never heard so fine a Voice. Her Notes so high. The Kettle Drums from Westminster Abbey sounded charmingly, beat by Mr. Ashbridge. (Diary for 1788))

Even more characteristic of the determination to establish findings upon this affair, to report upon it as on an alien form of activity, is the next passage from the same account.

Part II opened with a suite in F Major for orchestra (op. 39) by Moszkowski. This was much more clear and, in every way more interesting than the Beethoven; every now and then there were passages that were pleasing, not to say more. . . . I did not like the look of the young man who wrote it, and who also conducted. He had long yellowish hair and kept tossing his head to fling it back on to his shoulders, instead of keeping it short as Jones and I keep ours.

(*NB.* 132)

This is the tone of the Renaissance voyager finding strange customs among the anthropophagi. 'As Jones and I do ours': Jones is here quaintly brought in to fill out the picture of a society against which manners are to be measured. Butler, that is to say, distrusts the common standards too thoroughly to appeal to them against the length of Moszkowski's hair, though in fact they would no doubt have supported his reaction. 'Jones and I' are the largest society he can feel easy in quoting; for the rest of the audience he feels as a dog towards bullocks; they are potential enemies when they are not open ones.

What we have noticed in Butler's concert-going reactions has its bearing upon the whole direction of his work. For it may be agreed that the distrust which Butler felt for all accepted reputations which he had not managed personally to test, led him both to make his own conquests, or acquisitions, in literature, and elsewhere, too thoroughly his own —to work over them too minutely and repeatedly in his effort to rub them clean of all vestiges of previous ownership—and also to be liable to exaggerate the importance of those acquisitions and discoveries simply from the knowledge that they were his own. The list of his 'most interesting finds' in the note 'My Work' (Notebooks) leads the reader to this conclusion. The disproportion in value and interest between the successive 'finds' is remarkable. 'Finds' of potential importance, at least, for humanity, are not distinguished even by numerical order from 'finds' such as

10.   The restoration to Holbein of the drawing in the Basel Museum called 'La Danse'.   (*NB.* 376)

and

12.   The discovery of a life-sized statue of Leonardo da Vinci by Gaudenzio Ferrari.   (*NB.* 376)

Consideration of the mountain of activity (much of it unpublished) thrown up on the subject of the authorship and site of the *Odyssey* leads one to a similar conclusion. Nor do we feel this observation to apply only to the larger divisions of Butler's work. It may be felt as equally true of the detail as of the whole. There are certain of Butler's fancies in that characteristic mixed biologico-philosophical-satirical world which are felt almost at their first appearance to have no life in them, and yet which are reverted to as persistently as the obviously livelier ones.

The characteristics of the typically good Butlerian idea are first, that, while it breaks down accepted classifications at one point, it shall be sufficiently plausible for us to want to allow this if we can. Then it shall be an idea that will combine with and reinforce others of the same sort. Further, it shall have sufficient vitality and serviceability to apply in more than one kind of inquiry. The best of Butler's ideas turn up in different but recognizable shapes in connection with one then another of his interests—with the principles of morality, with evolution, with art, and so on. Butler is peculiarly the philosopher of the continuity of phenomena. This is one of the amateur philosophies with which we are familiar, and one out of which Butler more than ordinarily made capital. His habit was constantly to try out his ideas in new contexts, to substitute one idea for another, a remote one for an immediate one, to make an old idea work in a new situation. There is in the whole notebook method of composition at once the effort constantly to make new connections between distant ideas, and the assumption that the multiple application of certain ideas shows an actual continuity in the different sorts of natural phenomena. The connection is evident between this habit of mind and the methods of satire, with its mixing up of *worlds*, its concealment of one world behind another; and one is frequently conscious (in the books on evolution in particular) of Butler's advocating, with all the plausibility of the satirist, theories behind which there is in fact no ironic intention.

The contrast is therefore quite a marked one between those ideas of Butler's that are serviceable and lively, and certain others that seem unworkable from the start. The latter ideas lack the plausibility necessary to their kind; they do not set up any will to believe, to justify the violation that they do to accepted theory. They are not in themselves attractive ideas, and they do not cohere easily or naturally with the facts that they are intended to explain. The facts and the explanation lie stiffly side by side, and, in the absence of further demonstration of their connection, remain unjoined; there is a rigidity in the idea which facts and explanation together make up, that compels it to show but the one face whatever the context it occurs in. It is, in fact, for Butler a dead idea, yet he will sometimes run it as consistently as though it were a live one. I can think of several examples: the notion of Vibrations as the 'universal substance', which Butler runs in *Unconscious Memory* and elsewhere—here the flaw is in the literalness with which the notion is supported, the claim to an impossible scientific truth that is made for it: and again the notion that eating may be regarded as the enforcement of a stronger opinion upon a weaker, treated in *Life and Habit* and elsewhere—here it is the distance between the fact and the explanation which kills it, or at least turns it into an ineffectual little joke.

This uncertainty as to the probable serviceability of individual speculative ideas, as much as the lack of the more general sense of proportion between major interests, has its connections with the development in Butler of the sense of ideas as property. On 'Rosmini on Property' he remarks:

> He declared it to be a kind of extension of personality beyond the limits of the body. (*F.E.* 149)

and by corollary, ideas, being the extension of personality beyond the body, are property. One is occasionally tempted to say that the only cause under Heaven of Butler's not being a Baconian was the fact that someone had been one before him. But no more absolute a protection was necessary or could be imagined. The need for single and absolute possession is as real for him in regard to notions and tastes as it is in the details of his own life. We should remember that Butler would never allow himself to possess books (other than his own) and depended for all that he needed on the British Museum reading room. Clearly, to be surrounded by other people's books made him uncomfortable; they were so much parts of other personalities as to prevent him from ever making them altogether his own. In those rooms in Clifford's Inn, cluttered as they were with objects, their walls bedevilled with framed reproductions like those of an actor's dressing-room, everything had become a piece of Butler. He enumerated the articles to be carried in his ruck-sack, and Festing Jones recorded them in an appendix to his *Life*. His walks in the suburbs of London were traced in red ink on a map—an acquisition to be fixed, an extension of the personality to be perpetuated.

In all this emphasis upon Possession I find something that takes us back to the picture of Butler as he who had to steal his own birthright, and was punished for it.

> The Three Most Important Things a man has are briefly, his private parts, his money, and his religious opinions. (*F.E.* 93)

It is as though Butler had had to steal all three of these. And that he was, as he says, punished for it, seems equally true and clear. Though so tenacious, as we have seen, of all that he thought of as belonging to him, the mature Butler claimed noticeably little of life. There is something rather moving in the meagreness and dispirited tone of a note for the year 1882:

> Obscurity: The only two things I should greatly care about if I had more money are a few more country outings and a little more varied and better cooked food. (*NB.* 367)

The voice is that of a contented and industrious prisoner who is resolved to make the best of things. In 1895 this postscript is added:

> I have long since obtained everything that a reasonable man can wish for. (*NB.* 367)

If this convinces us of happiness, it is of one of only the most limited sort.

> I am anxious to have it generally known that I am well off, because if I were poor my history would be too depressing; because a cheerful figure is more attractive than a wronged and unhappy one; because, in fact, it leaves the laugh on my side. (*F.E.* 228)

It is the desire to appear happy, rather than the attainment of happiness, of which we are most conscious. The same thing is to be felt in *The Way of All Flesh*. The final 'happiness' of Ernest, to which so frequent references are made, remains as imprecise and unsupported by detail as the 'happiness' on which spirits 'on the other side' are wont to insist. Malcolm Muggeridge has said all that it is necessary to say of the ludicrous moment in *The Way of All Flesh* when Ernest returns to his parents' home, 'got up regardless of expense', and overwhelms his father with the news that he has inherited £70,000 from his aunt Alethea.

His year and a half of peace had effaced all the ill-effects of his previous suffering, and now that he had become actually rich there was an air of *insouciance* and good humour upon his face, as of a man with whom everything was going perfectly right, which would have made a much plainer man good-looking. (*W.O.A.F.* 379)

Here, of course, the essential absurdity of the situation, the crudity and obviousness with which the scene has been rigged up, make the picture of Ernest 'happy' altogether unacceptable. But let us take a more considered statement on the same theme.

To love God is to have good health, good looks, good sense, experience, a kindly nature and a fair balance of cash in hand. (*NB.* 33)

Note that the sole outward-going quality mentioned is in 'kindly'. Kindliness is the sole *épanchement*, and a typically restricted and narrow one. There is a dignity of a kind about the passage, one which depends almost wholly on the word 'kindly'; it is this word that alters the sense of the passage from one of contentment to one of regret and resignation. 'Kindly' alters the force of the 'good health,

good looks, good sense'; it reduces to little more than
triviality their claim to give value to life. Kindliness, one
feels, amounts here to 'not hurting others more than you
can help'; and the upshot of the passage is that this is about
all one can legitimately claim from life. It suggests more
than anything else the picture of the hero who has 'died',
and come to life again only a little: fearfully scarred,
blasted, and timid of claiming anything too much.

A note published in the *Further Extracts* has for me a
particular significance:

> There Will Be No comfortable and safe development of our social
> arrangements—I mean we shall not get infanticide, and the permis-
> sion of suicide, nor cheap and easy divorce—till Jesus Christ's Ghost
> has been laid, and the best way to lay it is to be a Moderate
> Churchman.   (*F.E.* 163)

The desire to shock that dictates the passage does not make
it the less remarkable how completely destructive and
negative the programme is. Butler's anarchism is so
genuine as to be unobtrusive. His adoption of the title of
Conservative in politics and his dislike of Liberals or
Radicals is really the indifference of the pure anarchist.
Infanticide, suicide and divorce are as self-contained a programme as liberty, equality and fraternity. The link
between them is the need that we have already noticed, the
need that people should not hurt each other more than is
necessary. To get rid of children by killing them is to
prevent them from hurting themselves or their parents, to
get an easy divorce is to enable two people to stop hurting
each other, to kill oneself is to put an end to self-inflicted
pain. The sense is that though there is not much that we
can do for people, we can at least try to limit their power
for hurting one another; and in this attitude there is a re-
flection of Butler's own refusal to make demands upon life.

Butler had a fear of appearing to complain which led him, one feels, at times to falsify the picture of his own situation. At least, there is a ring of truth in those passages where he does allow himself to appear as less than happy, that gives them a more than usual persuasiveness.

> I am well enough, but low and, as usual, clinging to ledges of precipices with light green slopes of easy pasture always well in sight and always eluding me, especially when I think I am closest to them. However, if there is anything of devil in my books, it is this which has in great measure put it into them.
>
> (Letter of 19 February 1884)

This quotation from a letter to Miss Savage carries an air of conviction and would no doubt have been true at most periods of Butler's life. It is the tone of the convalescent, and of the habitual rather than the temporary convalescent; the health that is hoped for is near enough to be visible, but is never completely reached. Butler's life should be seen as a sharp and heroic resistance to a nearly mortal illness followed by a restoration to an inevitably low and never quite secure state of health.

> Torrents and Annoyances are formed because rain drops can fall more quickly through the air than they can travel along the ground when they have fallen. The falling drops overtake the running ones and there is a block.
>
> So every annoyance must pass away in some small change, as a rain drop sinks into the ground; and it will do so if annoyance does not succeed annoyance too rapidly. As a general rule, the ordinary channels of action suffice to carry off the disturbances, whether pleasing or painful, of the hour, but every now and then there are, as it were, floods. *(F.E.* 150)

This may be taken as a key to the nature of Butler's personal anxieties. He says in his account of his relations with Pauli,

> If in my writings at this time there is something which the reader can feel but not grasp...it is due, I believe, to the sense of wrong

which was omnipresent with me, both in regard to Pauli, the Darwins and my father, and also to my ever-present anxiety as regards money. (Charles Paine Pauli and Samuel Butler. *Life and Letters*, October 1931, 226)

And in thinking of this statement, it is worth bearing in mind Butler's analysis of the nature of Annoyances. The danger of the flood, of the rising to a general and disastrous inundation of the latent sense of wrong, must continually have been present to Butler, and have been influential in leading him to a defensive limitation of his own demands. The strength of the sense of wrong may be felt to have something to do with the strength of the feelings that were involved for Butler in the initial assertion of his own personality, the throwing-off of the 'Langar' self. It no doubt involved an unreasoned sense of his own guilt as well as of that of others, and was, in fact, part of the 'punishment' which he describes as the result of his action. A reduction of his plan of life to that which involved the smallest amount of attachment or personal expectation was the best protection against attacks from such dangerous forces.

This self-denudation, this reduction of demands, had as one of its results, that of putting Butler in a very favourable position in the world of controversy. Obviously, a reduction to the minimum of one's own requirements is the best sort of backing for a destructive controversial position. Butler's special toughness in controversy is greatly a matter of his own successful detachment and renunciation. The personal example of how little in the way of accepted values can be got along with is the best sort of polemical weapon. Butler's freedom in the controversy upon evolution, his privilege to exaggerate and to have fun with his own theory, rests in the fact that for him the whole business does not really matter. He is at liberty to be in earnest upon his theory as far as it pleases him, and then to give it a twist into fancy or satire. Similarly, in the attack upon the Church, he can go, as he does in *The Fair Haven*, as near as he likes to the language of orthodox religious apology, in that if the irony goes wrong, and the book has the effect opposite to the one meant, it does not ultimately greatly matter.

A test for detachment and quietism is, of course, to be found in lack of public success, and it is one out of which Butler comes fairly well. In finding far-fetched reasons for thinking obscurity and lack of public approval a benefit, Butler is like any other unsuccessful author; for any one who takes his work seriously (which means in fact any one who writes at all) a degree of self-deception about the value of success must be pretty well unavoidable. And Butler rarely pretends that he does not take his work seriously. How much he was involved in it, and the pains which it laid him open to, may be seen from his admissions in *Unconscious Memory* upon the subject of 'Life and Habit'.

…though I could see no flaw in the argument, nor any loophole for escape from the conclusion it led to, yet I did not dare to put it forward with the seriousness and sobriety with which I should have treated the subject if I had not been in continual fear of a mine being sprung upon me from some unexpected quarter.   (*U.M.* 21)

Though my book was out in 1877, it was not till January 1878 that I took an opportunity of looking up Professor Ray Lankester's account of Professor Hering's lecture. I can hardly say how relieved I was to find that it sprung no mine upon me.   (*U.M.* 26)

This is fairly strong from one who had little in the way of a public reputation to lose. It effectively disposes of any fancy that we might have had for regarding Butler as a pamphleteer, an exponent of abundant lightly held opinions. The freedom and comparative unassailability of his controversial position did not at all derive from a personal insensibility to attack. The tone of his remarks upon public reactions to his work has as little detachment as those of any other unsuccessful writer:

Of course I should have liked it very much if *The Times* had taken a fancy to me; it would have put a lot of money in my pocket which in the old days I wanted very badly. At the same time I strongly suspect it to have been a good thing for me in the end that *The Times* should have let me so severely alone, and have long since resolved so to write in the future as to make this severity most likely to endure. (*F.E.* 278)

My Book On Shakespeare's Sonnets: *The Times* does not consider that it deserves to have attention called to it. Am I to be piqued at this, or should I not rather be proud of it? I have little doubt which of the two I ought to feel, and none as to which I do feel.... He who lets himself be chagrined by men who are either obviously incompetent or obviously insincere, deserves to be chagrined. (*F.E.* 325)

The inconsistency is perfectly natural and need surprise no one. What is more to the point is that Butler's chief answer to the problem of his lack of present success, his faith in the value of posthumous fame, attains with him quite a special force and power to convince.

When I thought of Buffon, of Dr Erasmus Darwin, of Lamarck, and even of the author of the *Vestiges of Creation*, to all of whom Mr Darwin had dealt the same measure which he was now dealing to myself: when I thought of these great men, now dumb, who had borne the burden and heat of the day, and whose laurels had been filched from them; of the manner, too, in which Mr Darwin had been abetted by those who should have been the first to detect the fallacy which had misled him; of the hotbed of intrigue which science has now become; of the disrepute into which we English must fall as a nation if such practices as Mr Darwin had attempted in this case were to be tolerated;—when I thought of all this, I felt that though prayers for the repose of dead men's souls might be unavailing, yet a defence of their work and memory, no matter against what odds, might avail the living, and resolved that I would do my utmost to make my countrymen aware of the spirit now ruling among those whom they delight to honour. (*U.M.* 49)

Coming from such a partisan position, and exaggerated in its condemnations as it probably is, this still seems to have an element of magnificence. The personal application, the claim for the same thing to be done for Butler's own fame after his death, does not destroy the effect of the passion with which he defends the fame of the Buffons and the Lamarcks. This is evidently not merely a way of belabouring Charles Darwin; however much or little the championship of the unjustly treated dead is genuine with regard to Buffon and Lamarck, one is left convinced of the efficiency of posthumous honour in general.

> Yet meet we shall, and part, and meet again,
> Where dead men meet, on lips of living men.

People say that living for posthumous fame is hollow. I cannot see that it is more hollow than living for the pleasures of life, or for anything else. If it affords satisfaction—and it does so for me—it is solid enough for all practical purposes.　　　　　　　(*F.E.* 245)

The world may prove hollow but a well-earned good fame in death will never do so. And all men feel this whether they admit it to themselves or no.

Faith in this is easy enough. We are born with it. What is less easy is to possess one's soul in peace and not be shaken in faith and broken in spirit on seeing the way in which men crowd themselves, or are crowded, into honourable remembrance when, if the truth concerning them were known, no pit of oblivion should be deep enough for them.　　　　　　　(*NB.* 361)

The theme constantly recurs, and the language grows in vehemence where it does so. It is Butler's ability to convince us of his satisfaction in this sort of fame which gives a balance and strength to his indifferentism or Stoicism.

For from Butler's Notebooks one can extract quite a comprehensive manual of Stoicism; it was a doctrine for which he developed a professional aptitude. The explicit

Hedonism in the same Notebooks continually suggests something like Stoicism underneath it. The doctrine of health, the doctrine of knowing one's own likes, the doctrine of moral compromise; in these there is at the most the top surface of Hedonism; the real substance is the doctrine of rejection, of avoidance of hurt rather than the courting of pleasure, of sitting quiet and not asking much, at least of the present life.

There is occasionally the attempt to give a rather more spectacular justification for an unspectacular mode of life.

There is no conception of the faith that a man should do his duty cheerfully with all his might though, as far as he can see, he will never be paid directly or indirectly either here or hereafter. Still less is there any conception that unless a man has this faith he is not worth thinking about. There is no sense that as we have received freely so we should give freely and be only too thankful that we have anything to give at all. Furthermore there does not appear to be even the remotest conception that this honourable, comfortable and sustaining faith is, like all other high faiths, to be brushed aside very peremptorily at the bidding of common-sense. (*NB.* 189)

The note is upon Bunyan. The attitude is one that attained a special prestige at the end of the Victorian period. It is the emotion of Fabianism: and one remembers the opportunist use which Bernard Shaw made of it from that period onwards. Butler, as we see, thinks it necessary to make a partial disclaimer as soon as he has stated the doctrine. And it is, indeed, as much too dramatic an interpretation of his general attitude, as the opposite version, the pretended rejection of duty, the tone of

I am so intent upon pleasing myself that I have not time to cater for the public. (*NB.* 372)

No view that does not involve posthumous honour as one of its benefits comes convincingly from Butler; a doubt about its value is hardly hinted at; and of the conscious renunciation of it he talks as of an almost impossible heroism.

It is here that faith comes in. To see that the infinite corruptions of this life penetrate into and infect that which is to come, and yet to hold that even infamy after death, with obscure and penurious life before it, is a prize which will bring a man more peace at the last than all the good things of this life put together and joined with an immortality as lasting as Virgil's, provided the infamy and failure of the one be unmerited, as also the success and immortality of the other. Here is the test of faith—will you do your duty with all your might at any cost of goods or reputation either in this world or beyond the grave? If you will—well, the chances are 100 to 1 that you will become a faddist, a vegetarian and a teetotaller.

And suppose you escape this pitfall too. Why should you try to be so much better than your neighbours? Who are you to think you may be worthy of so much good fortune? If you do, you may be sure that you do not deserve it. . . .

And so on *ad infinitum*. Let us eat and drink neither forgetting nor remembering death unduly. The Lord hath mercy on whom he will have mercy and the less we think about it the better.

(NB. 361)

The mercy of the Lord is here hardly at all more than posthumous fame. The Stoicism is of the unspectacular sort that comes most sympathetically from Butler.

CHAPTER II

'The Scratching of a Mouse'

BUTLER's attitudes have the effect of Stoicism more often than he means them to. An impotent doctrine of Hedonism —the advocacy of comfort and convenience and compromise, as we get it in the section 'Truth and Convenience' of the Notebooks—discloses clearly enough its Stoical foundation. The doctrine of not asking too much does not convince us of any background of enjoyment or success. It is in a far more unobtrusive manner that Butler's real capacity for enjoyment reveals itself. All through Butler's work there is a thin streak of a recognition of the enjoyable. He has an expert sense of the delightful and charming incident. I mentioned earlier the note of the convalescent in Butler. And that special capacity for the enjoyment of trifles, which one has at recovering from influenza, seems perpetuated in Butler's sensibility to the odd and pleasant thing.

> To them (Milton and Handel) an opportunity for a little paganism is like the scratching of a mouse to the princess who has been born a cat. Off they go after it—more especially Handel—under some decent pretext no doubt, but as fast, nevertheless, as their art can carry them. (*A. & S.* 249)

This is rather like a picture of Butler's own character, if one substitutes for 'paganism' his own more trivial and intimate sense of the delightful.

> I heard a woman in a 'bus boring her lover about the electric light. She wanted to know this and that, and the poor lover was helpless. Then she said she wanted to know how it was regulated. At last she settled down by saying that she knew it was in its infancy. The word 'infancy' seemed to have a soothing effect upon her, for she said no more but, leaning her head against her lover's shoulder, composed herself to slumber. (*NB.* 242)

There is the 'scratching of a mouse' here. An incident has
set up a pleasant irritation and Butler has pursued it to its
meaning. In a way it sets off the severity and painfulness
of Butler's general situation to realize, as in this, the degree
of his natural capacity for enjoyment, and the insignificance
of the material it needs to work on. In this sort of small
success one gets near to the real nature of Butler's talent.
His writing has a capacity for sharpness and penetration, of
quick combination of the elements of unremarked everyday
experience, which makes the success of the best things in
his controversial writings as much as in the Notebooks.

> And the bells in the windows of the campanile began, and I turned
> and looked up at their beautiful lolling and watched their fitful
> tumble-aboutiness. They swung open-mouthed like elephants with
> uplifted trunks, and I wished I could have fed them with buns.
> (*NB.* 266)

This is closely worked up, but still keeps the shape of the
original *find*. And one could wish that in *Alps and Sanctuaries*, which gave the best opportunity outside the Notebooks, Butler could have found a standpoint that left him
more continually at leisure to elaborate this sort of *find*. In
Further Extracts there is the note:

> I should like to write a book which should be like a picture with
> a deep Venetian blue-green sky and an impossibly rich, golden tone
> all over it. (*F.E.* 123)

Alps and Sanctuaries is no doubt his nearest approach to this
book. But the note suggests a mistaken idea of the real way
his talent was most likely to work. (One remembers George
Moore's desperate adventures in search of 'style', and the
unpleasant glaze of artificial language he spread over his
'Brook Kerith' and the other set pieces.) It is a relic of the
Pater influence on the period, and is relevant here, in that

it indicates how much Butler may have been led to under-estimate the value of his own ability for writing of quite another sort, the sort which proceeds by small and exact discoveries.

One or two more instances should be given of the sort of thing which I think Butler was so suited to do, and which best suggests the true impetus behind his more extensive writings. One comes from the Notebooks:

Eating Grapes Downwards

Always eat grapes downwards—that is, always eat the best grape first; in this way there will be none better left on the bunch, and each grape will seem good down to the last. If you eat the other way, you will not have a good grape in the lot. Besides, you will be tempting Providence to kill you before you come to the best. This is why autumn seems better than spring: in the autumn we are eating our days downwards, in the spring each day still seems 'very bad'. People should live on it a good deal; from the age of, say, fifty we eat our days downwards.

In New Zealand for a long time I had to do the washing-up after each meal. I used to do the knives first, for it might please God to take me before I came to the forks, and then what a sell it would have been to have done the forks rather than the knives. (*NB*. 99)

This is an elaborate exercise, and against it may be put a simple and more or less undeveloped fragment.

In An Italian Restaurant

Jones saw an officer who was finishing his dinner with a dish of little birds. A common soldier came in bringing a letter, and waited for an answer which the officer gave. This done he put a little bird on the end of his fork, told the soldier to open his mouth, put the bird inside it, and then went on with his dinner just as though he had been dropping a letter into a pillar-box. (*F.E.* 314)

By both of these quotations we cannot help being reminded of the most sympathetic picture we have of Butler, Miss Savage's description of him eating cherries in Berners Street.

One day when I was going to the gallery, a very hot day, I remember, I met you on the shady side of Berners Street, eating cherries out of a basket. Like your Italian friends you were perfectly silent with content, and you handed the basket to me as I was passing, without saying a word. I pulled out a handful and went on my way rejoicing without saying a word either. I had not before perceived you to be different from anybody else. I was like Peter Bell and the primrose with the yellow brim (*sic.*). As I went away to France a day or two after that, and did not see you again for months, the recollection of you as you were eating cherries in Berners Street abode with me, and pleased me greatly, and now it pleases me greatly to have that incident brought to my recollection again.

(Letter of 2 August, 1881)

It is typical of that discerning and attractive person to have seen the real value of Butler in this moment. From a dozen accounts of him, we see that odd, rather graceless figure that Butler cut in society—the 'enviably baggy trousers' that Desmond MacCarthy mentions and in which we see Butler equally prosaic and defiantly uneasy in a succession of photographs, looking suspiciously over his pince-nez at the terra-cotta figure of Stefano Scotto, or aggressive in the cave of Polyphemus; the 'sub-aggressive' air in the company of celebrated men; the dictatorial manner at Mr Heatherley's art classes, noted by J. B. Yeats in his *Recollections of Samuel Butler*; the fits of rage that he could only disguise by riding abruptly away into the bush, described by a fellow-colonist in his recollections of Butler in New Zealand; the coat that was desperately struggled into while the visitor waited at the door of his rooms in Lincoln's Inn; the general prickliness of behaviour in the visit to Trinity, sitting on a sofa, and saying nothing, 'letting them talk among themselves, and at 9.30 or soon after, when the master would be back...', creeping away 'as quietly as I could, feeling much bedraggled, and smaller by a good deal than I had done when I came—which doubtless is what the Trinity men intended'.

Yet when at his ease, and able to enjoy himself, one is made to recognize the special degree of *style* with which he was capable of acting.

How excellent and significant, as well as absurd, is the story that Desmond MacCarthy gives of his first meeting with Butler. The MacCarthys were staying at a hotel in Switzerland, and had been for some days aware of the formidable and slightly rebarbative-looking Englishman who sat near them in the dining-room. One evening, the little Desmond stayed out late and did not start on his way back to the hotel till after the proper time for dinner. Butler, seeing this from the window, went out to meet him and insisted upon taking him in to dinner in order to protect him from his parents. That Desmond might not need protecting from his parents could never, of course, have occurred to Butler, for whom his own personal experiences always had the force of general laws. Yet granting the essential absurdity, the action was both admirable and rather typical; there is a style, a grace, about it which cannot be ignored. And this faculty for the delicate small action is to my mind part and parcel of the sense for the small *find* of which I have been talking, the discovered trifle just beneath the surface of everyday life.

Muggeridge, in his general process of denigration, finds only an effort at self-aggrandizement in Butler's frequent reference to his servant Alfred. I do not think that he is here just, or that the 'Alfredisms' are the pawky professional jokes that come from a mere desire to have at all costs a comic servant. Alfred is a continual source of good jokes and genuinely odd remarks; and, indeed, the success of Butler's relationship with Alfred (Muggeridge's own interview with Alfred in his old age indicates how strong his feeling for Butler came to be) is the necessary standard against which to regard the fairly disastrous failure of his relationships with Pauli and Miss Savage, and the various degrees of unsatisfactoriness or misdirection which one observes in those with his literary opponents, with the Faesch brothers, and with Festing Jones.

There is something very pleasant in the typical Alfred remark.

Going up Fetter Lane one day with Alfred, I saw a fine dog, which I was going to pat, but Alfred stopped me, 'You had better be careful, sir,' he said, 'He's a business dog, and he may not like being spoken to.' (*F.E.* 320)

This is exactly the mild and queer little joke that Butler was expert in making and recognizing. He had the readiest response to idiosyncrasy and some of the resourcefulness of his best controversial style comes from the practice of catching the tone of the curious remark or the unnoticed *non sequitur*.

'Now, Sir,' said the clerk, 'you go to any of these famous dynamite people and ask them to throw you down that spire so clean on the middle of the roof as that is done. There isn't one of them as could do it. Lord bless you, sir, it's the hand.' (*F.E.* 302)

There is a lot of *The Fair Haven* in this. What is caught is the moment at which the disguised *wish* peeps through the theory. We remember the prayer at the end of one of Christina's reveries on the subject of Theobald and herself braving martyrdom at the hands of the Church of Rome.

'We, dearest Theobald,' she exclaimed, 'will be ever faithful. We will stand firm and support one another even in the hour of death itself. God in His mercy may spare us from being burnt alive. He may or may not do so. O Lord' (and she turned her eyes prayerfully to Heaven), 'spare my Theobald, or grant that he may be beheaded.' (*W.O.A.F.* 53)

The point is that there is a positive sense in which Christina is praying for Theobald to be beheaded; there is something actually pleasant in the idea of her husband suffering such a dignified and spectacular sort of death; and the likelihood or danger of such a thing happening assumes such force as her imagination gets into its stride that her own participation in the martyrdom is, as a precaution, gently excluded from the picture.

This is, of course, the whole theme of Christina in *The Way of All Flesh*, and gets more explicit treatment.

It was not for nothing that Ernest had been baptized in water from the Jordan. It had not been her doing, nor yet Theobald's. They had not sought it. When water from the sacred stream was wanted for a sacred infant, the channel had been found through which it was to flow from far Palestine over land and sea to the door of the house where the child was lying. Why, it was a miracle! It was! It was! She saw it all now. The Jordan had left its bed and flowed into her own house. It was idle to say that this was not a miracle. No miracle was effected without means of some kind; the difference between the faithful and the unbeliever consisted in the very fact that the former could see a miracle where the latter could not.

(*W.O.A.F.* 91)

Christina and Mrs Owen of *The Fair Haven* are the full exposition of the undisguised confusion of wishing and believing. Thus Mrs Owen

...several times...expressed to us her conviction that my brother and myself were to be the two witnesses mentioned in the eleventh chapter of the Book of Revelation, and dilated upon the gratification she should experience upon finding that we had indeed been reserved for a position of such distinction....Her notion clearly was that we were to be massacred somewhere in the streets of London, in consequence of the anti-Christian machinations of the Pope; that after lying about unburied for three days and a half we were to come to life again; and, finally, that we should conspicuously ascend to heaven, in front, perhaps, of the Foundling Hospital. (*F.H.* 13)

But Butler manages to catch in much less obtrusive and more intimate form the dilemma caused by the mixing up of personal desires, ambitions, necessities, and fears, with the business of belief and of theory. The devastating quotation from Mr Spurgeon is something seized upon by this sensitivity to the personal calculation behind the orthodox sentiment. Mr Spurgeon, in the course of a speech, prays to God to remove our rulers 'as soon as possible'. Mr Spurgeon's disastrous admission of scepticism is a consequence of his getting on such personal and intimate terms with the problems he should have left to his reason. Being a little uncertain about his belief in God, he attributes his own difficulty about believing to a quite different sort of difficulty, a social difficulty; God is assumed to be 'difficult', as a refractory child or a wealthy patron are 'difficult'. The propriety of apologizing to a busy, and possibly irritable, Deity for bothering him is, for Mr Spurgeon, so evident as quite to disguise the fundamental apology for want of faith. One is by now sick enough of the journalist's abominable phrase 'wish-fulfilment' and the unpleasant knot of misunderstandings that it represents. But if any exact meaning does lie behind the phrase, it must be something of the sort that Butler pins down in a chance overheard phrase or a mischievous quotation. Butler has his best claim to be scientific in his ability along these lines. The 'patient and careful' accumulation of evidence which was his favourite butt for jokes in the dispute with the Darwinians would not be an unfair description of his own method in this different sort of science. His Notebooks have quite an air of Victorian science in their scrupulous, systematic recording of the minor piece of evidence and the small discovery. When he notes that in a public conflagration people's sympathies are generally with the fire, and that they say 'the corner stack

46

is alight now quite nicely', the remark is not an isolated one; it gets its interest from reinforcing a dozen others and from corroborating a theory.

Mrs Jones's definition of science is a nice instance of the reverential version of science for which Butler blames the Darwins and the Wallaces, but it is not without its relevance to Butler's own case.

'Mathematics,' she explained, 'are not science, nor yet is astronomy; science consists of experiments, with lectures, but the main thing is the experiments.' (*F.E.* 320)

There is a direction in Butler's notes which reveals itself not only from reading the notes themselves in quantity but in the published writing for which they are the training.

From the note upon 'Imagination and Mistake' connections go out equally to the clerk's ideas on the collapse of the Shrewsbury spire—the seeing of what the observer wants to see—and to the Infancy of Electricity—where the familiar association gets the better of the indifferent fact.

Imagination and Mistake

Facts remain even now much at the mercy of the imagination which is their remote ancestor. If a man who is looking for his carriage in a railway station sees himself beckoned to by someone from a wrong carriage, he will certainly for a moment see the wrong carriage as his right one. So if we are looking along a railway expecting to see a train a long way off, and a man crosses the line also a long way off, we always at first take the man for the train. (*F.E.* 221)

It is, of course, a favourite theme with Butler, and he produces quite a mass of evidence: one often fails to notice that a man has grown a beard; William Sefton Moorhouse imagined he was being converted to Christianity by Burton's *Anatomy of Melancholy*, which he had got by mistake for Butler's *Analogy*. This training in the sense of the physical limits of thought, and the intrusiveness of the personal in any sort of rational consideration, has its use in developing Butler's scepticism about Darwin's 'theological' use of technical language.

But the experimentation which these notes represents has another bearing on Butler's style. For there is something of the scientific experimentalist in his constant trying-out of the new combination, the application to one study of the stored-up detail from another.

Dreams are a mode of parthenogenesis when the vibrations pre-existing in the brain vivify up to a certain point but do so all wrong as though in a mental ovarian tumour, through want of fecundation by incoming vibrations from exterior objects.   (*F.E.* 194)

There is a sharpness here which is a result of the notebook training. And, more generally, it is the constant note-taking activity which we see behind the characteristic agility in transposition, in substitution of terms, in sustained derangement of categories, which gives life to the speculative as to the satiric style. Butler's résumé of Buffon in *Evolution Old and New* has a liveliness which is not a matter of mechanical manipulation.

For our skull is a kind of flower-pot, and holds the soil from which we spring, that is to say the brain; our mouths and stomachs are roots, in two stories or stages; our bones are the trellis-work to which we cling while going about in search of sustenance for our roots; or they are as the woody trunk of a tree; we are the nerves which are rooted in the brain, and which draw thence the sustenance which is supplied it by the stomach; our lungs are leaves which are folded up within us, as the blossom of a fig is hidden within the fruit itself.   (*E.O. & N.* 137)

This, in a smaller way, improves upon its own initial mechanism, and gets a more general power over the imagination, as does the great passage in *The Tale of a Tub.*

The worshippers of this deity had also a system of their belief, which seemed to turn upon the following fundamentals. They held the universe to be a large suit of clothes, which invests everything; that the earth is invested by the air; the air is invested by the stars; and the stars are invested by the *primum mobile*. Look on this globe of earth, you will find it to be a very complete and fashionable dress. What is that which some call land but a fine coat faced with green? or the sea, but a waistcoat of water-tabby? Proceed to the particular works of the creation, you will find how curious journeyman Nature has been to trim up the vegetable beaux; observe how sparkish a periwig adorns the head of a beech, and what a fine doublet of white satin is worn by the birch. To conclude from all, what is man himself but a micro-coat, or rather a complete suit of clothes with all its trimmings? As to his body there can be no dispute; but examine even the acquirements of his mind, you will find them all contribute in their order towards furnishing out an exact dress: to instance no more; is not religion a cloak, honesty a pair of shoes worn out in the dirt, self-love a surtout, vanity a shirt, and conscience a pair of breeches, which, though a cover for lewdness as well as nastiness, is easily slipt down for the service of both.

The passage from Butler does in something of the same way make an assault upon the nerves; the attack upon the subject is constantly renewed and varied.

The Poor are compelled to work and use their muscles, and when there are no more poor there will ere long be no more muscles. The poor are a mode whereby the physical energy of the race is conserved.

(*F.E.* 200)

And again:

All our limbs and sensual organs, in fact our whole body and life, are but an accretion round and a fostering of the spermatozoa. They are the real 'He'. A man's eyes, ears, tongue, nose, legs and arms are but so many organs and tools that minister to the protection, education, increased intelligence and multiplication of the spermatozoa; so that our whole life is in reality a series of complex efforts in respect of these, conscious or unconscious according to their comparative commonsense. They are the central fact in our existence, the point towards which all effort is directed. Relaxation of effort here, therefore, is the most complete and comprehensive of all relaxations and, as such, the supreme gratification—the most complete rest we can have, short of sleep and death. (*NB.* 17)

The shock administered here is to an intimate part of the mind. Constantly, in the pursuit of an argument of a dubious, or at least fanciful, nature, a phrase with all the plausibility of satire halts us and gets an instinctive assent. One needs to be aware of the elements of Butler's view as to the relation of the unconscious memory of often repeated actions to physical growth, to feel the particular relevance of the following remark upon 'Structure and Instinct'. Yet assent to the theory has nothing to do with the immediate assent demanded by the image.

A structure is, as it were, a kind of internal bird's nest made in pursuance of an instinct. (*F.E.* 160)

This belongs to the world of satire, though it has a perfect relevance to a more or less serious theory. There is the telescoping of worlds that is one of the satisfactions of satirical writing.

CHAPTER III

The Writings on Evolution

PLEASURE, the 'scratching of a mouse', is the best key to Butler's writings on evolution. Butler's theories of the identity of instinct and memory, of cunning as the means of organic modification, of the continuity of memory between parents and offspring, are all so delicately balanced, and tremble so continually on the brink of nonsense, that there comes always the moment when he cannot resist going the one step too far. The training in plausibility got from the writing of satire, and from the elaboration of the notebook observation, makes the opportunity for a flourish, the temptation to see how much he can get away with, something not to be resisted. And on the whole, it is these moments, or the expectation of these moments, which really makes the virtue of this part of his writing. Postulating that the identity of individuals consists in their respective memories, he shows that in consequence, to eat something is to impose the eater's memories upon the thing eaten—and now the touch that finally sends the theory over the edge:

there is no such persecutor of grain, as another grain when it has fairly identified itself with a hen. (*L. & H.* 137)

This is quite fun, but it has nothing to do with biology. The theory has ceased to be a refutation of Darwinism; the world of writing is too different. Butler's natural defence is to make of this nothing more than a piece of decoration; but, in fact, it is the logical end of his theory. For it is the whole *nature* of Butler's theories which takes them out of competition with the theories which they are intended to oppose.

The personal dispute with Darwin showed the two men altogether at cross-purposes. The details of this foolish little dispute are well known and need not be repeated at any length. An article by Dr Krause upon Erasmus Darwin, published in Germany before the appearance of Butler's rehabilitation of the earlier Darwin's reputation in *Evolution Old and New*, was republished by Charles Darwin after the appearance of Butler's book, in an English translation, and with certain interpolations that had an evident reference to, and were a strong condemnation of, the view expressed by Butler on the subject of Erasmus Darwin. Darwin, in a preface, appeared to vouch for the unaltered condition of Dr Krause's article, and the resulting appearance was that the view contained in *Evolution Old and New* had been dismissed by Krause as an unimportant piece of 'mental anachronism' before it had even been proposed by Butler. The evidence produced by Festing Jones and Francis Darwin suggests convincingly enough that the fault on Darwin's side was at the most nothing more than that of carelessness, and the proportions which the incident subsequently took in Butler's mind, together with the failure of Darwin to take the easiest way of settling the difference, were clearly the result of their inherent inability to understand one another. Butler would have been perfectly satisfied with a published apology or explanation, and Darwin was willing to have given him one. What Butler could not conceive was that Darwin was really too frightened of him to attempt a public explanation. Butler's reputation as a destructive satirist was, in fact, quite a formidable one, and one need not doubt the genuineness of Darwin's timidity in the face of a dispute of a kind for which he was temperamentally ill-equipped; and if Butler could have imagined that a writer of Darwin's standing should in fact feel 'like a condemned prisoner' at the mere thought of such a dispute, the affair would have gone no further. As it was, Darwin offered a stiff and rather inadequate private letter of explanation, and when this was rejected by Butler, allowed himself to be persuaded by friends to leave any repetition of the charge unanswered 'as being unworthy of his notice'. Butler, of course, only too prone to suspect conspiracy and deliberate persecution, took this as confirmation of his suspicion; and the erroneous pictures which the two men had formed of each other hardened into something like the truth.

As men, Butler and Darwin were bound to misunderstand each other, and as writers they came to be almost equally at cross-purposes. For Butler's whole attitude to writing was too remote from Darwin's for there to be much real conflict or even contact between their views. The main charge remains true, that Darwin writes scientifically and that Butler does not. Yet for that reason the difference between their attitudes has more than a temporary interest. Darwin is generous of facts and niggard of theory; Butler founds an abundance of confident theory upon other people's facts. But that *Life and Habit* and *Luck or Cunning?* are so fertile in hypotheses and so exclusively theoretical in form should not disguise the fact that Butler's attempt is not to settle, but to unsettle. For all that his view is so full of positives, the positive element is there to discredit the few and tentative positives of *The Origin of Species*, rather than for any other purpose; or if that perhaps overstates the case, it is at least true that the *value* of the four books on evolution is almost exclusively a negative, a destructive one.

For the question most necessary to ask is, where it would take us if Butler's theories of growth and evolution were demonstrably true. Beyond Butler's theories on the biological subject there is the imminent danger of a dead-end. The germ of Butler's views is to be found in his theory of unconscious memory. According to this, the unconscious ease with which an often-repeated action is performed—the automatic facility with which a violinist can perform the most complicated operations, operations which if he attempted to perform with a full consciousness of what he was doing he would find of impossible difficulty—is to be taken to be identical with the unthinking assurance with which more truly instinctive actions are performed—say, a bird's building of its nest—and furthermore, identical with the method by which operations even lower than the rank of actions are performed, operations such as growth. A man is to be thought to grow his own limbs in something of the same way in which he walks upright or in which he plays the violin; that is, he does it only because he has learnt to do it, and does it so unerringly because he has done it so many times before and remembers unconsciously how to do it. He grows an ankle so much less consciously than he plays the violin, only because he has learnt to do it so much earlier, and therefore so much more completely.

But if he can remember how to grow an ankle, that is, if he can recall a time at which he learnt step by step how to do it, his recollection must clearly go back much further than is generally assumed, and the conclusion must therefore be that memory of some sort must be transmitted unimpaired from parent to offspring. (The memory that is so transmitted will of course be of one sort only, that of unconscious memory.)

The best way to enforce this assumption is to assert that the *identity* of individuals consists exclusively in their memory, and that if it can be shown that *identity* is not necessarily cut off by death, then memory also need not be thought to be interrupted by it. There is generally thought to be a continuous identity between the child and the man, and the embryo and the child. There should, therefore, not be more difficulty in allowing an identity between the spermatozoa and the embryo, and the parent and the spermatozoa. Identity, that is, is to be seen to continue uninterrupted from generation to generation—and if identity, then memory.

This is ingenious enough in itself, and is more ingeniously supported. And even from so bare a summary are to be seen obvious corollaries to characteristic personal attitudes of Butler's. If death is not to be thought the final interruption of identity, then to die in obscurity is not necessarily to die a failure. The life after death, the life of posthumous fame, with which we have already seen Butler to be obsessed, is brought pleasantly closer when death is deprived of its finality.

But what is more relevant to my immediate point is that, however ingeniously and amusingly Butler elaborates his theory of memory, he cannot convince us of more than that something rather *like* memory explains the processes of growth. The importance of assenting to, or dissenting from, Butler's theory is altogether diminished when it is realized that, however much similarity to the operation of memory the processes of growth may exhibit, we should never be justified in assuming that at any further stage where we have *no* evidence the similarity would continue. We know too much about memory to accept that it is memory pure and simple which is to be postulated as the principle behind growth, and any paring-down of the meaning of the word memory leaves us only with something *like* memory, something to be *compared* with memory, as the nearest thing to it.

Here we have what I mean by the dead-end. In *The Origin of Species* we have one kind of hypothesis, the working hypothesis, which may be used as far as it is useful, and abandoned when it ceases to be. Darwin's hesitation in committing himself to any one hypothesis, and the apparent theoretical vacillation which Butler seizes upon, represents a trained suspicion of the value of the over-neat hypothesis. The value of what Butler is doing seems to me to lie in the taking of a plausible hypothesis, and running it as far as it can possibly be made to go, with the effect of producing a case at once complicated, highly improbable, and apparently watertight, and which by its very neatness and conclusiveness brings out the more evidently its own inherent uselessness. For to construct a theory at once ingenious, plausible, and useless, has the effect of discrediting the whole business of scientific theorizing.

No doubt Butler did not consciously regard the matter quite in this way. None the less, the feeling grows upon one that what Butler is doing in his work upon biological subjects is to take an oblique revenge upon the whole contemporary scientific movement. Darwin in the '60s was an overwhelming influence upon young writers. We have Butler's own word in the introduction to *Unconscious Memory*, as to the extraordinary sway which Darwin assumed.

There is no living philosopher who has anything like Mr Darwin's popularity with Englishmen generally; and not only this, but his power of fascination extends all over Europe, and indeed in every country in which civilization has obtained a footing; not among the illiterate masses, though these are rapidly following the suit of the educated classes, but among experts and those who are most capable of judging . . . in England and Germany there are few men of scientific reputation who do not accept Mr Darwin as the founder of what is commonly called 'Darwinism', and regard him as perhaps the most penetrative and profound philosopher of modern times. (*U.M.* 2)

And the power which the movement exercised over Butler at this period must have been comparably great. Nothing more natural then, for Butler, than a rebellion against the completeness of the authority which the movement initially gained over him. And it is interesting to see how almost his first adult exercise in writing, the paper to a New Zealand journal which subsequently became *Darwin among the Machines*, was, to his own surprise, taken as a rebellion against Darwin. At the time he denied, and sincerely, that the article had been so intended; but the rest of his career shows that this was in fact the hint for his most effective criticism of the Darwinian theory.

At the time, of course, it was the apparent unassailability of the Darwinian position that made it fun to play tricks with it. The Darwinian theory seemed for the moment so safe, securer against effective attack, indeed, than most of the Christian doctrines, that a fanciful perversion of the theory seemed a harmless enough affair. It was only later, when Darwinism had sufficiently come of age for its initial overwhelming influence to have waned, and the degree to which it was a partial and tentative combination of hypotheses, rather than a secure and complete revelation, had become apparent, that the force as criticism of the approach represented by *Darwin among the Machines* was revealed.

Butler's approach to the matter was from the beginning a theological one. The account which he gives of it in *Unconscious Memory* is of considerable interest. Facing the question of evolution itself, as distinct from Darwin's contribution to the theory of how evolution could operate, Butler finds two alternatives. Either Darwin had deliberately ignored the problem of the creation of the original germ of life from which all other living beings had evolved, or he intended it to be assumed that life was not in fact distinguishable from matter and had in some way been evolved from matter. Taking the second alternative, he says:

I first asked myself whether life might not, after all, resolve itself into the complexity of arrangement of an inconceivably intricate mechanism. (*U.M.* 13)

Kittens think our shoe-strings are alive when they see us lacing them. Cats, though not taken in by shoe-laces, may be by a toy-mouse.

Suppose the toy more complex still, so that it might run a few yards, stop, and run on again without an additional winding up; and suppose it so constructed that it could imitate eating and drinking, and could make as though the mouse were cleaning its face with its paws. Should we not at first be taken in ourselves, and assume the presence of the remaining facts of life, though in reality they were not there? Query, therefore, whether a machine so complex as to be prepared with a corresponding manner of action for each one of the successive emergencies of life as it arose, would not take us in for good and all, and look so much as if it were alive that, whether we liked it or not, we should be compelled to think it and call it so; and whether the being alive was not simply the being an exceedingly complicated machine, whose parts were set in motion by the action upon them of exterior circumstances; whether, in fact, man was not a kind of toy-mouse in the shape of a man, only capable of going for seventy or eighty years, instead of half as many seconds, and as much more versatile as he is more durable? If then, men were not really alive after all, but were only machines of so complicated a make that it was less trouble to us to cut the difficulty and say that the kind of mechanism was 'being alive', why should not machines ultimately become as complicated as we are, or at any rate complicated enough to be called living, and to be indeed as living as it was in the nature of anything at all to be? (*U.M.* 13)

As I have said, Butler did not at the time realize the full implications of this:

I do not suppose I at that time saw that this view comes to much the same as denying that there are such qualities as life and consciousness at all, *and that this, again, works round to the assertion of their omnipresence in every molecule of matter,* inasmuch as it destroys the separation between the organic and inorganic, and maintains that whatever the organic is the inorganic is also.   (*U.M.* 14)

And it is to this second conclusion that Butler does indeed come. If it is to be either all mind or no mind, we might as well plump for all mind.

The only thing of which I am sure is, that the distinction between the organic and the inorganic is arbitrary; that it is more coherent with our other ideas, and therefore more acceptable, to start with every molecule as a living thing, and then deduce death as the breaking up of an association or corporation, than to start with inanimate molecules and smuggle life into them; and that, therefore, what we call the inorganic world must be regarded as up to a certain point living, and instinct, within certain limits, with consciousness, volition, and power of concerted action.   (*U.M.* 15)

What is evident is that Butler has pinned down Darwinism to something very much like materialism either way. If there really is to be no distinction between the organic and the inorganic, if it is to be all life or all mechanism, then it clearly does not much matter which we choose. The life, the 'consciousness, volition, and power of concerted action' which is to be attributed to plants and stones, is not sufficiently like the accepted idea of life to be of much comfort to anybody; it is as distinct a conception, however much it may possess the same symptoms, as the memory which is to be attributed to the cells of the ankle-bone is distinct from the approved notion of memory.

Butler faces the evolutionist with two versions of existence, each equally incompatible with anything that has the right to call itself religion. In rehabilitating mind as the force behind organic modification, he imposes so frigid and so insignificant a meaning upon the word 'mind' as to make his rehabilitation more detrimental to orthodoxy than the rejection of mind which he proposes as the alternative. And in this way, Darwinism is brought into the very difficulties with the religious world which Darwin himself was anxious to prevent.

The impression left by *The Origin of Species* is that Darwin, writing in an age of religious controversy, made it his deliberate aim to incur the very minimum possible of conflict with religious opinion. The clear statement of an evolutionary theory at all was bound to be a shock to the religious part of the public, but, apart from that, his whole effort was to justify a claim for science to pursue its inquiries independently of religion. Butler himself has shown how religion had impeded and complicated previous attempts to state a theory of evolution, and how Buffon was forced to express himself obliquely, by equivocations, and by hints concealed amid passages of a quite different and orthodox tenor. And one is aware all the time of Darwin's sense of how much difficulty and awkwardness religion is liable to introduce into a discussion of this sort, if given the chance, and of his constant effort to avoid religious territory, and, where possible, to placate the religiously inclined by an occasional pious and agreeable epithet. 'Beautiful' is the most characteristic adjective in *The Origin of Species*; we are referred to 'the beautiful adaptations in nature;—such as the long neck of the giraffe for browsing on the branches of trees'; we read of 'that perfection of structure and co-adaptation which justly excites our admiration'. In the final paragraph we have, indeed, a mild but explicit confession of faith:

...There is grandeur in this view of life, with its several powers, having been originally breathed by the Creator into a few forms or into one; and that, whilst this planet has gone cycling on according to the fixed law of gravity, from so simple a beginning endless forms most beautiful and most wonderful have been, and are being evolved.

In all this, though no doubt sincere, one should see the plea of the scientist to be left alone; there is to be, as it were, a gentleman's agreement between the Church and science that each shall let the other be.

Of course, the wish was not granted, and the conflict of Huxley and Bishop Wilberforce was only one incident of a prolonged and violent struggle. Yet it was inevitable that in this conflict Huxley should have been the victor; for against the immediate orthodox protest the Darwinian position had a clear and safe enough line of defence. A straight fight between religion and science was an energetic affair, but it left either side more or less uninjured; the Church was used to that sort of thing, and so was science, and after a little while the two parties might have got on again pretty amicably.

The effect of Butler's intrusion upon the scene was quite different. In *Darwin among the Machines* he had found the proper way to make things awkward for the Darwinians. Attack the theory from the outside and it can defend itself without much discomfort; but go inside the theory, follow up its suggestions to their logical conclusion, make amendments to the theory so as to give it a dubious sort of compatibility with religion, and the defenders of the theory are irretrievably committed to what they most wished to avoid, a discussion upon theological ground.

It might be noted here how much of Butler there is in the passage about the toy-mouse. The suggestion is inescapable that Butler is so ready to envisage 'a toy-mouse in the shape of a man, only capable of going for seventy or eighty years' because the possibility not only does not give him any great discomfort, but in fact offers a certain kind of satisfaction. If the toy were sufficiently complex, 'Should we not at first be taken in ourselves, and assume the presence of the remaining facts of life, though in reality they were not there.' We recognize, first, the readiness to assume a wholesale fraud on the part of Nature. One remembers that Darwin was even a little shocked at the idea of insects imitating the appearance of flowers unless it could be proved that the deception was forced upon them. But for Butler, to be taken in was quite the likeliest thing to occur to one; his own career presented itself to him in the shape of a series of wholesale frauds—from his father's religion to the 'patient and careful' inquiry of the scientists—to which he had nearly or completely succumbed. And one can imagine that there might be a sort of relief in the notion of escaping from yet another, and an even more wholesale, deception. I am reminded of the fancy in *Life and Habit*, which I have already quoted, of human beings as parasites upon a giant creature of another race, into some other part of which, at our death, we should re-enter 'starting clean anew, with bygones bygone, and no more ache for ever for either age or antecedents'. To someone feeling upon these lines, the notion of animated nature as one extensive and complete fraud would carry at least enough prospect of pleasure for him to envisage it with composure.

On these lines we may be able to account for another development of Butler's view which seems, at first sight, surprising. To support the attribution of memory to the cells of the body, and indeed to every living thing, as in *Life and Habit*, it is clearly likely to be a convenience if a definition of memory can be found which gives it an equal applicability to this remote species of memory and to memory in the accepted sense of the word. Accordingly, in

Unconscious Memory and more fully in *Luck or Cunning?*, Butler proposes a theory of vibration as the basic constituent of memory. His statement of the theory has the ingenuity that one expects, and is worth quoting at some length:

Our conception, then, concerning the nature of any matter depends solely upon its kind and degree of unrest, that is to say, on the characteristics of the vibrations that are going on within it. The exterior object vibrating in a certain way imparts some of its vibrations to our brain—but if the state of the thing itself depends upon its vibrations, it must be considered as to all intents and purposes the vibrations themselves—plus, of course, the underlying substance that is vibrating. If, for example, a pat of butter is a portion of the unknowable underlying substance in such-and-such a state of molecular disturbance, and it is only by alteration of the disturbance that the substance can be altered—the disturbance of the substance is practically equivalent to the substance; a pat of butter is such-and-such a disturbance of the unknowable underlying substance, and such-and-such a disturbance of the underlying substance is a pat of butter. In communicating its vibrations, therefore, to our brain a substance does actually communicate what is, as far as we are concerned, a portion of itself. Our perception of a thing and its attendant feeling are symbols attaching to an introduction within our brain of a feeble state of the thing itself. Our recollection of it is occasioned by a feeble continuance of this feeble state in our brains, becoming less feeble through the accession of fresh but similar vibrations from without. The molecular vibrations which make the thing an idea of which is conveyed to our minds, put within our brain a little feeble emanation from the thing itself—if we come within their reach. This being once put there, will remain as it were dust, till dusted out, or till it decay, or till it receive accession of new vibrations.

The vibrations from a pat of butter do, then, actually put butter into a man's head. . . . The same vibrations, therefore, form the substance remembered, introduce an infinitesimal dose of it within the brain, modify the substance remembering, and in the course of time, create and further modify the mechanism of both the sensory and motor nerves. Thought and thing are one.   (*L. or C.* 310)

This is as lively and amusing as the best passages of *Life and Habit* (I am inclined to think *Luck or Cunning?* the most amusing of the four books), but is not so plausible. 'Vibrations' itself has a suspicious air of jargon—the very scientific jargon upon which Butler was elsewhere so severe—and the whole passage has more than a trace of jargon. 'The same vibrations...modify the substance remembering, and in the course of time, create and further modify the mechanism of both the sensory and motor nerves.' Whatever meaning there might be behind this is blanketed by its phraseology. It is very unlike Butler's normal style, and makes one suspect an attempt to cover a confusion of thought. For, when one looks more closely at the passage, there appears a considerable amount of bluff about it. 'Molecular disturbance', 'feeble', 'infinitesimal dose' are all a kind of bluff. To put this theory of vibrations in terms of feebleness and strength is to make it look familiar; but at no point is it conceivable that we should ever come to *feel* what it means for a 'feeble' emanation from a pat of butter to exist in our mind. Why 'feeble'?—It is because 'feeble' is a way of introducing a possibility of complexity into what would otherwise appear altogether too simple, bald and inadequate a reduction of the nature of perception. 'Feeble' is a way of explaining how the natural order can be reversed to the extent of butter being introduced into the head; a 'feeble' emanation of butter is near enough to no butter for it to be credible, much as it was found that an infinitely slow evolution was hardly a more shocking conception than no evolution. But when any other criterion is applied to the word 'feeble', when it is asked, for instance, whether the feebleness or strength of the dose of butter can be calculated mathematically, the true absurdity of the epithet becomes clear. Butler, of course, was hardly likely to have been unaware of this. He himself apologizes for the theory:

> I commend these two last speculations to the reader's charitable consideration, as feeling that I am here travelling beyond the ground on which I can safely venture; nevertheless, as it may be some time before I have another opportunity of coming before the public, I have thought it, on the whole, better not to omit them, but to give them thus provisionally. (*L. or C.* 312)

I have said that the theory of vibrations was a surprising development of Butler's view, because from the beginning the notion might have been seen not to be of the kind sympathetic to his amateur approach. The passage I have quoted is the most amateurish-sounding in the four books, and it is so from the very presence of the professional, technical pretension. 'Vibrations' is a notion chosen for its equivocal suggestions—half-way between mind and matter. It is like the popular idea of a spiritual apparition, something made of ectoplasm if possible, and if none is available, of cheese-gauze as the next best thing. For the average observer, as long as he has no very exact idea of what cheese-gauze is, and does not meet with it anywhere else, there is not much choice between the two materials. In either case, the aim is a something as much like nothing as possible. Not that it is to be suggested that Butler was alone in this sort of pursuit. The history of philosophy shows a whole series of vortices, atoms, *élans* vitals and so on, that are the result of the search for a compromise between something and nothing, between physical and non-physical. But Butler was too literally minded to be satisfied with the kind of working fiction to which philosophy is apt to give these names. When he wrote 'Vibrations' we can take it for granted he really meant something that could literally be called vibrations, and not merely something for which the word was a convenient sign. The single-mindedness, the insistence upon the single, naked meaning of words, of which he makes a virtue in his attacks upon the language of theology or upon Darwin's casuistical definition of 'Natural Selection', leads him here to try to make us *feel* what he means by 'Vibrations', and the result is a signal enough failure. And it is surprising, for it throws away some of the advantage that he has hitherto gained by fairness and literalness, and by the careful playing of his best card, the accomplished *literary* sense of what can and cannot be said. Before anything else, the passage is bad as literature.

The curious ways in which the emotional situation of a writer will influence even the details of his intellectual system have been so often illustrated that we ought not to be surprised if some element in Butler's personal attitude favoured the development of this unfortunate theory of Vibrations. It certainly fits in with our picture of Butler that he should have been ready to accept a circumscribed and mechanical explanation of human phenomena; there is here something of the stripping, the avoidance of excessive demand, which we have noticed in his writing upon humane topics.

If it is wished to indicate the essential difference between Butler's and Darwin's approaches to the subject of evolution, it cannot be done better than by considering the following quotation:

The distinctive feature was not due to any deep-laid plan for pitchforking mind out of the universe, or as part of a scheme of materialistic philosophy, though it has since been made to play an important part in the attempt to further this; Mr Darwin was perfectly innocent of any intention of getting rid of mind, and did not, probably, care the toss of sixpence whether the universe was instinct with mind or no—what he did care about was carrying off the palm in the matter of descent with modification, and the distinctive feature was an adjunct with which his nervous, Gladstonian nature would not allow him to dispense. (*L. or C.* 294)

Putting on one side the imputation of disingenuousness, this is a very fair statement of Darwin's attitude. Darwin really was, or wished to be, indifferent to the theological consequences of his theories, since he knew very well how capable they were of diverting him from the central object of his inquiry. Butler's persistently theological approach was, as has been seen, the one most calculated to interfere with this plan, and to make things difficult for the Darwinians. But Butler would anyhow have been committed to some such approach, by reason of something more fundamental than a limited prejudice against materialism. Butler was incapable of sustaining any partial critical attitude towards the objects of his attacks; his charge against his opponents always grows and becomes wholesale as the discussion continues. This characteristic is well described by Hugh Kingsmill:

The proselytising part of Butler's nature was always quarrelling with his subtle and deep sense of reality.... It did not content him to state his views in the certainty that persons to whom these views were congenial would be helped by him to grasp them more fully. His aim was to force theologians, scientists, and professors to recant opinions, for the expression of which in the past they had been handsomely paid, and for the elucidation of which they would continue to be rewarded. Nor was it only their material well-being which Butler expected them to sacrifice. He required them, in effect, to readjust their whole relation to reality, to destroy the laboriously-erected structure of their self-respect, and, in short, to inform the world that they had hitherto been talking nonsense.

(*After Puritanism*, 73)

Butler was, of course, aware of his own tendency. Ernest Pontifex, it may be remembered, decides while still in prison that his fellow-countrymen must be persuaded for their own good to leave off believing in the supernatural element in Christianity:

> Looking at the matter from a practical point of view he thought the Archbishop of Canterbury afforded the most promising key to the situation. . . . There must be an amount of cogency which even an Archbishop—an Archbishop whose perceptions had never been quickened by imprisonment for assault—would not be able to withstand. When brought face to face with the facts, as he, Ernest, could arrange them, his Grace would have no resource but to admit them; being an honourable man he would at once resign his Archbishopric, and Christianity would become extinct in England within a few months' time. (*W.O.A.F. 292*)

By occasional admissions, Butler allows it to appear that his assault upon Darwin, and his professed intention to force him by *coup de main* to a total recantation, is not meant altogether seriously. There are momentary relaxations of the attack here, much in the same way as by an occasional flash of sympathy for Theobald, in *The Way of All Flesh*, he shows his awareness that the passionate condemnation of his father in his picture of Theobald is true only for him, and that for other people his father might be the genuinely honourable and attractive person they thought him. And it is when the attack upon Darwin has become the unmitigated personal assault of *Luck or Cunning?*, in which the results of eight years' calculation of the surest and quietest ways to be offensive are collected, that his campaign becomes most amusing, and most valuable.

The difference between what Darwin and what Butler are doing is so complete, that it should be possible to enjoy Butler's attack without allowing it to alter one's picture of Darwin. Butler is concerned to explode the legendary character of the dispassionate scientist with his 'patient and careful' accumulation of evidence; and Darwin's constant

reference to a body of experimental evidence which is the
necessary support for the theory in hand but which lack of
space prevents him from producing, can readily be made to
appear irritating, if not something more. Yet if ever anyone
had a claim to the character of the patient and minutely
laborious man of science, it must be Darwin. What an
extraordinary picture of a man *The Origin of Species* gives.

> I forced many kinds of seeds into the stomachs of dead fish, and
> then gave their bodies to fishing-eagles, storks, and pelicans; these
> birds, after an interval of many hours, either rejected the seeds in
> pellets or passed them in their excrement; and several of these seeds
> retained their power of germination.   (*Origin of Species*, Ch. XII)

He floats the dried branches of asparagus on water to test
the possibility of their seeds' crossing the ocean in a fertile
condition. He cuts out portions of a geological map of
a certain colour and *weighs* them to ascertain their proportion to the whole. The capacity for method shown in such
casual details is something fabulous.

On the other hand, when Butler objects to the language of
The Times of 1886 in saying that 'Mr George Romanes
appears to be the biological investigator on whom the
mantle of Mr Darwin has most conspicuously descended',
there is some point in the objection. The 'mantle' of
Darwin, the reputation as a methodical investigator to
which he had so indisputable a claim, could be, and he
persuades us that it was, altogether too easy to claim by
writers of quite another temper of mind. There is no better
illustration of the dangers which the new movement in
biology, and the new lustre given to the biological
investigator, carried with it, than the preface written in
1910 by Professor M. Hartog to Butler's own book *Unconscious Memory*. Hartog is concerned to show that Butler
'receives from an official biologist of the first rank full

recognition for his wonderful insight and keen critical power'. In 'official biologist' we have the full strength of Butler's objection to the authoritative pretensions of the Romaneses and the Ray Lankesters of his own day.

Here are one or two quotations from Hartog's 'official' biologists:

> The general fact is that the organism reacts by concentration upon the locality stimulated for the *continuance* of the conditions, movements, stimulations, *which are vitally beneficial*, and for the *cessation* of the conditions, movements, stimulations *which are vitally depressing*.
>
> (Dr J. M. BALDWIN, *Development and Evolution*)

> Here we gain on one side a deeper insight into the imprint action of stimuli. It reposes on the lasting change in the conditions of the living matter, so that the repetition of the immediate or synchronous reaction to its first stimulus (in this case the stooping of the boy, the flying stones, and the pain on the ribs), no longer demands, as in the original state of indifference, the full stimulus *A*, but may be called forth by a partial or different stimulus, *B* (in this case the mere stooping to the ground). I term the influences by which such changed reactions are rendered possible, 'outcome-reactions', and when such influences assume the form of stimuli, 'outcome-stimuli'.

After this, Butler's attention to the *language* of scientific discussion has an obvious justification.

The central charge against Darwin was that he had confused the doctrine of evolution itself, of which he had no claim to be the originator, with his own contribution to the doctrine, the suggested *means* of evolution. And in the first edition of *The Origin of Species*, Butler traces ninety-seven passages in which a personal claim is made to ownership of the general evolutionary theory of descent, including forty-five uses of the actual word 'my' in connection with the theory. Of these forty-five, thirty-six had been excised by the edition of 1872, thirty 'my's' being cut out in a single

'Stampede of my's' in the fifth edition, as a result, so Butler suggests, of the appearance of Haeckel's *History of Creation*, in which an attempt was made to rehabilitate Lamarck's contribution to the evolutionary theory. Further, having in the first edition of *The Origin of Species* left himself more or less committed to a theory of the *accidental* or spontaneous arising of those variations in type upon which natural selection was to be thought to work in producing new species, Darwin persisted against increasing difficulties in defending this view, since it provided the best claim to distinction from the teaching of Erasmus Darwin, who favoured the theory of design or need as the cause of variation.

> Though Mr Darwin, if he was to have any point of difference from his grandfather, was bound to make his variations accidental, yet, to do him justice, he did not like it. Even in the earlier editions of the *Origin of Species*, where the 'alterations' in the passage last quoted are called 'accidental' in express terms, the word does not fall, so to speak, on a strong beat of the bar, and is apt to pass unnoticed. Besides, Mr Darwin does not say point blank 'we may believe', or 'we ought to believe'; he only says 'may we not believe?' The reader should always be on his guard when Mr Darwin asks one of these bland and child-like questions.... (*L. or C.* 99)

As an example of the sort of difficulty into which it is to be supposed that Darwin fell, and of the way in which he was forced to exculpate himself, Butler quotes from the same paragraph:

> Further, we must suppose that there is a power represented by natural selection or the survival of the fittest always intently watching each slight alteration.... (*L. or C.* 99)

Of this he says:

> Mr Darwin probably said 'a power represented by natural selection' instead of 'natural selection', only, because he saw that to

talk too frequently about the fact that the most lucky live longest as
'intently watching' something was greater nonsense than it would be
prudent even for him to write, so he fogged it by making the intent
watching done by 'a power represented by' a fact, instead of by the
fact itself. As the sentence stands it is just as great nonsense as it
would have been if 'the survival of the fittest' had been allowed to
do the watching instead of 'the power represented by' the survival
of the fittest, but the nonsense is harder to dig up, and the reader is
more likely to pass it over.   (*L. or C.* 100)

Butler pursues this through the various editions of Darwin's
book, and finds in the three most important editions the
three following variants:

1859: Further, we must suppose that there is a power always
intently watching each slight accidental alteration....

1861: Further, we must suppose that there is a power (natural
selection) always intently watching each slight accidental alteration.

1869: Further, we must suppose that there is a power represented
by natural selection or the survival of the fittest always intently
watching each slight alteration....   (*L. or C.* 101)

Butler remarks of these:

The hesitating feeble gait of one who fears a pitfall at every step,
so easily recognizable in the 'numerous, successive, slight altera-
tions' in the foregoing passage, may be traced in many another page
of the *Origin of Species* by those who will be at the trouble of
comparing the several editions. It is only when this is done, and the
working of Mr Darwin's mind can be seen as though it were the
twitching of a dog's nose, that any idea can be formed of the
difficulty in which he found himself involved by his initial blunder
of thinking he had got a distinctive feature which entitled him to
claim the theory of evolution as an original idea of his own.
                                                    (*L. or C.* 101)

'The twitching of a dog's nose', Darwin's 'nervous,
Gladstonian nature', his 'happy simplicity', are good and
convincing digs. The catching of Darwin's voice is done

maliciously, and no doubt unfairly, but none the less successfully. And there is more to it than that. Allowing for the fact that the imputation of deliberate disingenuity is pretty certainly unjustified, there still seems to me a great value in the sort of attention that Butler gives to the language of scientific writing, and the possibilities of mystification of which it is apt to make use. Of Darwin's defence of the expression 'Natural Selection', Butler says:

> For my own part I know of few passages in any theological writer which please me less than the one which I have above followed sentence by sentence. I know of few which should better serve to show us the sort of danger we should run in if we were to let men of science get the upper hand of us.　　　(*E.O. & N. 368*)

This is the sort of criticism he is able to enforce without any competence other than that of a man of letters, and his analysis of the passage in question is unmistakably useful. There is a constant need for someone who will make use of his literary position to expose vicious tendencies in the style of non-literary writings. What is required is the Arnoldian ear for a *tone of voice*; and it is in something of Arnold's manner that Butler displays how the tone of a defensive paragraph or over-qualified sentence may be made to reveal a dishonest intention in an argument.

CHAPTER IV

Butler and Miss Savage

IN the first part of this work I have treated the topics which are indispensable to any study of Butler, and all that is directly relevant to my attempted reassessment of his work is to be looked for in the three chapters composing this section. In the succeeding chapters I mean to deal less methodically with certain secondary topics. These chapters should, indeed, be regarded as little more than appendices to the main argument; they are discursive in character (perhaps to an unjustifiable degree), and claim attention simply as the record of certain quite personal impressions of Butler's personality and relation to his period. The topics are such as have caught my interest, and are not introduced with any pretence of completeness. Certain elements of both the life and the work (for instance, Butler's relations with Pauli, and the Homeric studies) I shall more or less ignore, though they are of no small interest. As subject of the first of these notes, I shall take the matter of Butler's relations with Miss Savage.

The letters between Butler and Miss Savage had always seemed the most attractive part of Festing Jones's *Life of Butler*, and the correspondence as it has since been published by Cape, in a single volume, with Butler's own comments, is not disappointing. Most of those who have read her letters have agreed in finding Miss Savage a delightful person. One would like to know more about her; though indeed there was probably little enough to know, and that by now certainly beyond discovery.

Butler has been frequently and severely blamed for the clumsiness that he showed in his dealings with her; but whilst the clumsiness has to be admitted, I think it unnecessary to pity Miss Savage in this respect. The pity which her story must necessarily arouse is that of a more general regret at so much talent mixed with obscurity so complete and sufferings so constant. As for her relations with Butler, I have no doubt that all the misunderstanding was on Butler's side. Miss Savage impresses me as a person capable of defending herself against any serious damage from her relations with so self-revealing a person as Butler. No doubt she may, as Jones suggests, have wanted to marry him in the first place; but she did not need to marry Butler to understand him, and her letters show almost from the beginning so thorough a knowledge of the way to handle him, her teasing and encouragement are done in such a clever and balanced manner, that I doubt whether the pain that Butler was convinced of causing her by his physical indifference to her played any important part in her life. Festing Jones, whose account of the matter is otherwise convincing enough, says

So their friendship drifted on, she offering him all she had to give, he taking all he wanted and making such return as he could, but despising himself, unhappy and discontented because he could not give the one thing which he believed her to be asking.... (*F.J.* 1, 445)

In 'she offering him all she had to give' there is a trace of the same assumption that we object to in Butler's own attitude. It is a sort of comic bachelor's conviction that fun and easy friendliness and wit on a spinster's part can only be a superior sort of husband-hunting and are to be treated with as much suspicion as Miss Tox's pin-cushion. 'Granted that she oppressed me with her very brilliancy' says Butler himself, '—nay bored me, for there is no bore like a brilliant bore....' Butler in his constant reference to her brilliance is making the same suggestion—that she was making a peculiar effort for him, that she was putting herself out. 'Brilliancy' suggests a studied display, a sort of Hannah-More-ism such as she would particularly have loathed (she found George Eliot unreadable for this reason). Enjoyment and sense of pleasure, much more than brilliance, are the real characteristics of her letters, and the error of both Butler and Jones seems to me to lie in ignoring the right of such a person as Miss Savage to get enjoyment out of the relationship for its own sake. It is, indeed, the most essential criticism of Butler's conduct in the matter, that he failed to enjoy the relationship with Miss Savage.

... she rarely left my rooms without my neck swelling and my head for a time being all wrong.

It was evidently Butler's conscience that made his neck swell, rather than Miss Savage. The theology of Langar had left him with that capacity to plague himself with rights and wrongs which was so often fatal to his sense of enjoyment. One finds the nature of the struggle, that made these meetings of such violent discomfort to him, in the three late sonnets. It is the true Puritanical expertness in self-laceration; he exasperates his nerves by enacting imaginary and disagreeable embraces under the compulsion of duty.

The misinterpretation of Miss Savage's words 'I wish you did not know right from wrong' is characteristic. Right and wrong were terms as natural to Butler in this connection as they were unnatural to Miss Savage; his mind worked upon them constantly and self-mortifyingly, playing upon them as in the second sonnet:

> A man will yield for pity, if he can,
> But if the flesh rebels what can he do?
> I could not. Hence I grieve my whole life long
> The wrong I did, in that I did no wrong.

76

In *Erewhon Revisited* family relationships are relaxed and family rights largely abandoned, or at least inverted. And in the desire for that state of affairs can be seen Butler's own dread of the rights that others may claim over him. It was, of course, Butler's fatal propensity to imagine rights over him that perpetuated the extraordinary entanglement with Pauli; and it was awareness of his own propensity in this direction that led to the elaborate precautions against sexual entanglements. It was fifteen years before 'Madame', the prostitute of his Tuesday afternoon visits to Islington, came to know Butler's name and address. And the alarm which Miss Savage's 'brilliancy' inspired in him has an odd parallel in Lytton's *The Coming Race*, a utopian satire contemporary with *Erewhon*. In Lytton's underground utopia the women are the dominant race, and make the sexual advances; and Lytton suggests that the campaign for Women's Rights, of that period, had as its real object the assertion of the right of women to propose marriage to men. No doubt Butler shared Lord Lytton's nightmare. Rights had a fascination as well as a horror for him.

The pain seems mostly to have been on Butler's side, therefore; Miss Savage strikes one as a most undemanding person, and, I should think, succeeded both in guessing Butler's own attitude and in enjoying the relationship notwithstanding it. Her tone throughout the correspondence is perfectly balanced; it is Butler who, from time to time, forces the tone. He has a sudden access of brusqueness or chilliness when it comes to making an appointment with her; he gets into a fearful and unnecessary moral tangle about the disposal of her letters. He is constantly worried about the basis of the relationship, whilst she is content to accept it for what it is. In the case of the letters, indeed, he succeeds in annoying her. First of all he tells her he is burning her letters. Then, deciding that this has hurt her, he tells her that he is keeping them. Then he becomes conscience-stricken about keeping them, and makes elaborate arrangements for their return to her at his death; and in general, he treats her letters as some sort of high explosive. To make matters worse, he remarks that he has the fancy that the letters of hers which he has burnt had been written with more care than any of the subsequent ones. Her reply is rather admirable:

With Care! This Side Up!

Dear Mr. Butler,

It must be confessed that I am a most unreasonable person. What! I leave off writing 'with care' when I hear that you don't keep my letters, and I don't write at all when you tell me that you do! Well, it only shows that I am a true Erewhonian, and have studied in the schools to good purpose. But you are mistaken when you talk about my being hurt when you told me you burned my letters. On the contrary I felt relieved, and I am sure you can have only a very hazy recollection of the matter, or you would not have recalled a very unpleasant moment of my existence.

And now, my dear Mr. Butler, let me give you a little good advice. If you wish to make yourself agreeable to the female sex, never hint to a woman that she writes or has written 'with care'. Nothing enrages her so much, and it is only the exceptional sweetness of my disposition that enables me, with some effort, I confess, to forgive this little blunder on your part.

As a matter of fact, I don't care what becomes of my letters. Keep them, or burn them as you please, only for goodness sake don't label them to be returned to me at your death. If you do, I shall never write to you without thinking of your death, and that I cannot bear to think of. Besides, you assume that I shall live the longest, which is flattering to my vital forces, but suppose I die first? What will become of my letters then? Pray let every contingency be prepared for and provided against while we are arranging the matter....

(Letter of 15 September 1877)

Butler even then does not perfectly take the lesson—that it
is irritating to have it suggested that she is concerned to
know what happens to her letters, and that, by corollary,
she writes them with an eye to some ulterior purpose—and
later remarks ingenuously thàt Jones always enjoys her
letters. To this Miss Savage replies with justifiable
irritation that she does not *always* write to Jones.

These are the only two occasions on which Miss Savage
allows herself a little bad temper with Butler—she had
both the provocation and the ability to be a great deal more
severe—and though Butler clearly assumed that on these
occasions she was hurt, I doubt whether she was in fact
anything more than annoyed.

Capacity for enjoyment has its bearing upon this relationship in more than one way. For what made Miss Savage so
excellent an influence on Butler as a writer, and what made
it such an overwhelming stroke of luck for Butler that she
should have entered his life when she did, was her ability to
suggest her enjoyment of his writing. To have had his
writings admired was what he might readily have expected
from any friendly disposed acquaintance; to have someone
insist upon her *enjoyment* of them, constantly to demand to
see more of them, and to pretend that her interest in his
welfare and health proceeded entirely from the desire to
have as much more of his writing as possible—this was
quite a different, and an infinitely more valuable sort of
encouragement. The enjoyment was clearly genuine; she
got a keen pleasure out of his humour, she liked to imitate
his 'wickedness' and did it well enough for him to borrow
from her, her ruthlessness towards his enemies was quite
as single-minded as his; she delighted in Gladstone-
baiting, and complained of the stupid safety of Portland
Place which allowed Gladstone to cross the street

undamaged; she talked fretfully about the mildness of the weather and in the same breath politely inquired about the health of Butler's father. Moreover, she knew precisely the direction Butler's writing should take, and did her utmost to guide him that way. Butler could have found no better critic; at every point her influence is unmistakably for good. It was Miss Savage who continually encouraged him in the writing of a novel. He confessed himself that nothing had given him half as much difficulty, or led him so often to despair, as *The Way of All Flesh*; and I have little doubt that it was Miss Savage's admirably flattering way of insisting upon the pleasure that each fresh chapter of the novel gave her, and her constancy in asserting him to be a born novelist, which supported Butler through the endless revisions of the story that he found necessary. It was Miss Savage, too, who put her finger upon the cause of the later chapters' failure, who pointed out the essential absurdity of the Miss Maitland episode, and objected to the priggishness of the mature Ernest. She objects to Townley: 'A coarse creature with vicious propensities which he indulges in a slum. . . .' She disapproves of the idealization of Aunt Alethea (drawn largely from herself, as she no doubt was aware):

I think you make the aunt a little ridiculous when you say that she preferred to encourage others rather than paint or write herself. When people don't do things themselves it is either because they couldn't if they tried, or because they are lazy, or because they have something else to do, or because they are morbidly vain. . . . You make her like that most odious of women, Mrs John Stuart Mill— who, though capable of surpassing Shelley preferred to efface herself for the greater comfort of Mr John Stuart Mill! At least that is what he was so extraordinarily simple-minded as to be taught to believe.
(Letter of 6 December 1883)

Lame, plain in an age whose clothes accentuated plainness, more or less penniless, living with uncongenial parents, having as her most intimate friend a 'dear good silly little chirrupy lady artist', Eliza Savage made for herself all the independence of spirit and rational freedom that Butler to the end failed of possessing. We are uneasy about Butler's probable death-bed utterances as we should never have been about Miss Savage's, even had we not known her last recorded words to have been a desire to support the School Board, 'for the noise the children made had, she said, prolonged her illness for at least forty-eight hours, and she was determined to crush all the vitality out of them'.

CHAPTER V

Erewhon Revisited, The Coming Race and *News from Nowhere*

Where sympathy (fellow-suffering) is preached nowadays and, if I gather rightly, no other religion is any longer preached—let the psychologist have his ears open; through all the vanity, through all the noise which is natural to these preachers . . . he will hear a hoarse groaning, genuine note of self-contempt. It belongs to the over shadowing and uglifying of Europe, which has been on the increase for a century . . . if it is not really the cause thereof.

(NIETZSCHE, *Beyond Good and Evil*)

BEHIND the poverty and tentativeness of Butler's values the 'hoarse, groaning, genuine note of self-contempt' is as audible as it is behind the philanthropical socialism which Nietzsche has chiefly in mind. The passion of *Erewhon Revisited* is in a way the passion of self-contempt. Self contempt here takes the form of prostration before the Child. Hugh Kingsmill said of this book: 'Higgs, returning to Erewhon twenty years or so after his first visit, is no longer Higgs but Butler in search of a son.' This perhaps rather over-dramatizes the case; no doubt the bearing is not as directly personal as this would suggest; none the less it points in the right direction. Immolation before the idea of the Child is traceable in Butler's work before *Erewhon Revisited*. The attribution of the authorship of the *Odyssey* to Nausicaa, to an adolescent girl, had as a part of its attraction the chance to magnify the claims of youth and innocence against experience—'experience', of course, representing Butler's perennial enemies, the established authorities. It is a familiar preoccupation of Butler's. The theory of *Unconscious Memory* was made to

82

bear the suggestion of the superiority, the authority, of the young. The young have their memory in a perfect state; they thrive because they know what to do; *all* their progenitors must at least have passed through adolescence or they could not have been progenitors, therefore the adolescent have an unbroken chain of memory of the actions suitable to their age, and are perfectly fitted to perform them; they are, as it were, perfectly wise, as compared with the middle-aged, who are doing what only a proportion of their forebears have lived to do, and with the old, who are doing what only a few of their forebears have done, and are consequently uncertain, and unwise, in their conduct of life. Growing old, according to this theory, is a process of unlearning inherited wisdom.

Again, in the book on the sonnets of Shakespeare, the whole endeavour is to prove that Shakespeare was not more than adolescent when he wrote them. The argument for this theory is indeed of another sort. Shakespeare has to have been young when writing the sonnets, because only of a young man are the faults admitted therein (faults consequent upon a disreputable entanglement with a young actor) excusable and reconcilable with the admiration that is to be paid to Shakespeare. But the interest in Shakespeare as a young man is a symptom of the general preoccupation with the claims of the young.

In Lord Lytton's *The Coming Race*, a book which appeared at about the same time as *Erewhon* (*Erewhon* was for a time attributed to Lytton) there are several interesting sidelights upon Butler. Lytton's utopian fantasy is a naïve piece of period writing, something in the Jules-Vernian manner and written in the main as a piece of entertainment, but it none the less carries several recognizable themes of Butler's and Morris's attempts in the same genre. The

'Coming race' are a people concealed under the earth and separated from the rest of mankind during a widespread inundation. By reason of the greater difficulties which they have had to overcome in order to live, they have reached (upon Lytton's characteristic version of the Darwinian principle) a stage of development considerably in advance of the dwellers on the surface of the earth. Scientific advance has been consummated in the invention of a physico-psychological power called 'Vril', which is described rather in the terms of an advertisement for a patent-medicine, and which has superseded all other forms of power—it runs machinery, burns as a fuel, rives mountains, enables the coming race to fly, paralyses or kills as a long-range weapon—and 'Vril', contained in a staff, being in possession of every citizen, masculine superiority in power has declined and women have become the dominant sex. The hero, the invader from the upper world, is consequently from the beginning in the condition of a helpless and child-like victim. He suffers considerable embarrassment from the advances made to him by the females of the new race—both because it shocks his sense of propriety and because if any of them were to insist upon adopting him as a husband he would be liable to the death penalty for being party to an unnatural union—but what is more to our point, the strongest relationship that he makes is with a boy, Tae. Tae is friendly to him, but as father to son. He is tender to the hero; he instructs and advises him and takes him about with him as a kind of pet; when the hero becomes refractory, the boy reminds him of his helpless state by the use of the 'Vril' staff. Finally, Tae is given the job of destroying the hero because of the interest which he has been unlucky enough to arouse in one of the women of the community; and there is a pathetic scene between Tae and the hero ending in an escape.

The bearing of this is that in a utopia, where mastery over nature is complete, and where, consequently, political organization admits of universal equality and the effective cultivation of idleness and amenity, the differences between age and youth disappear almost as much as the differences between the sexes and the classes. The occupation of the typical nineteenth-century utopia is the cultivation of innocent enjoyment, and for that the child is as well fitted as any one. The extraordinary juvenility of the world of *News from Nowhere* and that of *Erewhon Revisited* is a logical consequence of the initial assumption of a settled and unquestioned political system. In Lytton's new world things are so settled politically that nobody has much to do but indulge in aerial sports upon their 'Vril'-directed wings.

In their own way they are the most luxurious of people, but all their luxuries are innocent. They may be said to dwell in an atmosphere of music and fragrance. Every room has its mechanical contrivances for melodious sounds, usually tuned down to soft-murmured notes, which seem like sweet whispers from invisible spirits...in all their sports even the old exhibit a childlike gaiety. Happiness is the end at which they aim, not as the excitement of a moment, but as the prevailing condition of the entire existence; and regard for the happiness of each other is evinced by the exquisite amenity of their manners.

This fantasy of innocent luxury is what the average person connects peculiarly with the word 'utopia', and the thing most noticeable about it is the juvenility of the life that it represents.

In reproducing this familiar and popular version of the utopia Lytton is hardly doing more than draw upon a fashion of the period. But when we come to a more serious exploitation of the notion of juvenility, as in Morris's *News from Nowhere*, where it is evident that the writer has some stronger reason for a preoccupation with the innocent and the childlike, it is as well to remember the *necessary* connection between the utopia and the childlike in literature.

The immediate impression left by *News from Nowhere* is that it is written by a bluestocking. Indeed I have always felt that Morris's verse reads like that of a talented poetess. And *News from Nowhere* has a feminine sprightliness of tone that would make it pass easily for the fancies of a suffragette in the provinces. The world of this book is a hopeful and cheerful affair; universal love turns up as a clear bubbling stream of good spirits. Everybody smiles and laughs a great deal (they do this in *Erewhon Revisited* also). Dick, the oarsman says:

the fellows used to chaff me at one job where I was working, I remember, and sing out to me, 'Well rowed, stroke!' 'Put your back into it, bow!' 'Not much of a joke,' quoth I. 'Well,' said Dick, 'everything seems like a joke when we have a pleasant spell of work on, and good fellows merry about us; we feel so happy, you know.'

Social relationships are delightfully easy; St Winifred's and St Hilda's are ransacked for a suitably innocuous slang: 'Dick old fellow', 'Ne quid nimius! Don't overdo it', 'Well lads, old and young'. We have here permanently the indiscriminate friendliness that one had associated with an Evangelical bible-reading just before the reading. The supposition of feminine authorship would do a lot to explain the tone of this society. There is an attitude to Progress which seems peculiarly feminine; private houses in this society combine the conventions of the model factory and Renaissance Gothic. Terra-cotta friezes, marble mosaics, open timber roof, arches, healthy Vita-glass windows and everything 'trim and clean and orderly and bright'. People always prefer this kind of thing when they have any sense of architectural power, 'because then they know that they can have what they want, *and they won't stand any nonsense from Nature in their dealings with her'*. This is entirely the Stern Little Housewife motif. Dick, too, wears a girdle which he has worked himself, and he takes from it a little silver bugle-horn and blows 'two or three sharp but agreeable notes on it'. The insistence that even the sound of Dick's bugle shall be agreeable betrays the gross domestic ideal of Everything of the Best; and one has the strongest conviction that Dick has one hand-worked girdle for weekdays and another for Sundays. Trimness, orderliness and brightness—the housewifely values; and added to these a doctrine of innocent enjoyment, of innocuous debauch.

> The spirit of the new days, of our days, was to be delight in the life of the world; intense and overweening love of the very skin and surface of the earth on which man dwells, such as a lover has in the fair skin of the woman he loves.

Somehow one feels that this 'skin of the earth' is so very clean and innocent and hygienic that one could, in the land-lady's phrase, eat one's dinner off it.

But the theory of feminine authorship will not do on its own. The feature ultimately most important about the world of Morris's book is its deliberate juvenility. 'Administration' says someone in the book, 'and organiza-tion, to use *long-tailed words.*' In this conscious running away from adult values you have the central theme. Easy automatic friendship, a lot of boating, and some jolly haymaking; it is the dream of the half-holiday from school. And the incidents in *News from Nowhere* all have the air of the child's charade. The relations between the sexes are those of the game of 'Mothers and Fathers'. Dick the oarsman with his little silver-toned bugle and his girdle is a child dressed up as an adult.

In the characters of George and his family in *Erewhon Revisited*, Butler has reached from different causes a point rather similar to Morris's in his *News from Nowhere*; he proposes, in something of the same way, a rest from masculinity and from adulthood. To show the similarity of the world of *Erewhon Revisited* to that of Morris, we may point to a detail in itself of no great weight. When the boy George gets the better of the professors Hanky and Panky, and holds over them their own threat of the 'Blue-Pool', Panky bursts into tears and begs for compromise. Here we have an evident trace of the *dressing-up* motif; Panky is a child dressed up as a Professor. The triumph of the youthful George recalls those stories for boys that appeared after the Great War in which the German agent is defeated by a schoolboy. The climax of the personal drama in *Erewhon Revisited* is another application of the triumph of the boy hero. Higgs has all along felt an acute sense of inferiority in the face of his own son; he sounds George at their first meeting as to the extent of the expiation which George would require of his father before admitting his title to that name; and upon George's agreeing to a bargain by which he is committed to forgiving his father if the latter will come back to Erewhon and confess his identity publicly, Higgs offers George his hand: George takes his father's hand (ignorant, of course, of whose hand it is he is shaking) 'doubtfully and somewhat disdainfully, but he did not refuse it'. (The 'doubtfully and somewhat disdainfully' puts one in mind of the response to a caress of a thorough-bred horse.) The 'groaning note of self-contempt' continues to the moment of the revelation of Higgs's identity to George.

'What have I done to deserve so much goodwill?' says Higgs, 'I have done you nothing but harm?' Again he was quite overcome. George patted him gently on the hand, and said 'You made a bet and you won it. During the very short time that we can be together, you shall be paid in full, and may heaven protect us both.' (*E.R.* 214)

So does George forgive his father. The issue is crucial; it is the relations of father to son that matter, and other relationships are accordingly reduced in importance; the Mayor, who marries Yram after Higgs had deserted her, is not expected to feel vindictively towards Higgs, and in fact does not so feel. Between Higgs and Yram their early affair is a mild little joke; and Yram feels, of course, no jealousy for Arowhena, for whom Higgs deserted her, and sends her the warmest messages. The whole preoccupation of Higgs is with his relations towards the children of Yram's household, and the necessity for their forgiving him.

My father was delighted with all of them, for they made friends with him at once. He had feared that he would have been disgraced in their eyes, by his having just come from prison, but whatever they may have thought, no trace of anything but a little engaging timidity on the girls' part was to be seen. The two elder boys—or rather young men, for they seemed fully grown, though, like George, not yet bearded—treated him as already an old acquaintance, while the youngest, a lad of fourteen, walked straight up to him, put out his hand, and said, 'How do you do, sir?' with a pretty blush that went straight to my father's heart. (*E.R.* 272)

What Higgs seems really to be asking to be forgiven for is simply his not being a child.

George belongs to the Lad school of literature. The Lad seems to have come into literature soon after Butler began his writing career. It is probably significant that George was a Ranger of the King's forests; it is not the only place in which you can see in literature the approaches of the Boy Scout movement. Housman, of course, gives us the classical examples of the Lad school. It is worth while, when thinking of Housman, to bear in mind those lines of Dr Johnson on which he perhaps drew:

> Wealth, my lad, was made to wander,
>   Let it wander where it will;
> Call the jockey, call the pander,
>   Bid them come and take their fill.
>
> Should the guardian friend or mother
>   Tell the woes of wilful waste,
> Scorn the counsel, scorn their pother,
>   You can hang or drown at last.

After Dr Johnson's hanging or drowning, it is easier to see the romantic nature of Housman's jail and hanging. And the jail in which Housman's Ned lies, representing, as it does, 'Trouble' or 'Shame', has a connection with the situation of Higgs. A preoccupation with 'golden lads', 'cans of ale', 'playing the man', has a lot to do with a prostration before the child; it is a way of asking forgiveness from the world of the preparatory school for a weight of heavy though undefined guilt. Housman is concerned all the time with exculpation; his expenditure of sympathy upon the unlucky country boy, the soldier in the unknown grave, the 'Roman and his trouble', is a kind of exercise in expiation for a confusedly felt personal guilt.

We may take another poem of the 'eighties, Hopkins's *Brothers*:

> ...When Shrovetide, two years gone,
> Our boys' play brought on
> Part was picked for John,
> Young John: then fear, then joy
> Ran revel in the elder boy.
> Their night was come now; all
> Our company thronged the hall;
> Henry, by the wall,

Beckoned me beside him:
I came where called, and eyed him
By meanwhiles; making my play
Turn most on tender byplay.
For, wrung all on love's rack.
My lad, and lost in Jack,
Smiled, blushed, and bit his lip;
Or drove, with a diver's dip,
Clutched hands down through clasped knees—
Truth's tokens tricks like these,
Old telltales, with what stress
He hung on the imp's success.
Now the other was brass-bold:
He had no work to hold
His heart up at the strain;
Nay, roguish ran the vein.
Two tedious acts were past;
Jack's call and cue at last;
When Henry, heart-forsook,
Dropped eyes and dared not look.
Eh, how all rung!
Young dog, he did give tongue!
But Harry—in his hands he has flung
His tear-tricked cheeks of flame
For fond love and for shame.
Ah Nature, framed in fault,
There's comfort then, there's salt;
Nature, bad, base, and blind,
Dearly thou canst be kind;
There dearly then, dearly,
I'll cry thou canst be kind.

In reading this our admiration struggles with our embarrassment; the intention seems to be deliberately to embarrass the reader; violent attraction struggles with violent repulsion in both reader and writer. There seems to be at work a sort of homeopathic process, an effort to obtain a release from the awkwardness of a situation by a determined rubbing-in of the awkward elements thereof. The cant, the sophistication of language—the cultivation of naïveté, as in 'old telltales', 'the imp's success', 'brass-bold', 'Young dog, he did give tongue',—it is a process of self-mortification and of attempted exculpation. And the properties greatly remind us of the scene of Higgs and the children: here again are the blushes, and the timidity; here again is the child's charade.

In literature, innocence is frequently the cloak for terror and panic. The contortions which writers impose upon themselves in presenting innocence are a familiar and perennial amusement. It has often seemed to me an amusing fact that Milton's Eve

> . . . as a *veil* down to the slender waist
> Her unadorned golden tresses wore.

Why must she have a veil? Or why should she yield

> . . . with coy submission, modest pride,
> And sweet reluctant amorous delay

when Milton goes on to insist upon the absence, in Eden, of shame:

> . . . dishonest shame
> Of nature's works, honor dishonorable,
> Sin-bred . . . ?

Milton is assertive and emphatic here because he is in difficulties. And the difficulty is one that goes deeper and is more inextricably entangled in the Lad vein of literature of the 'eighties. The Lad is Innocence, and however much the homeopathic method is applied to the material of this world of juvenile innocence, the difficulty remains. W. H. Auden, who made what one may believe was the final assault upon this territory, Auden of

> Success my dears—Ah!
> Rounding the curve of the drive
> Standing up, waving, cheering from the car,
>   The time of their life:
> The fags are flushed, would die at their heroes' feet;
> Quick, someone, tug at that handle, get
> At them shouting, shoulder them high, who won by
>   their pluck and their dare.

and of

> Sandroyd—what of their side?—
> In jerseys of chocolate and white
> Prancing for prowess, posh in their pride, unbeaten
>   last night.

still fails to take us beyond our embarrassment.

The root of the matter is that the homeopathic style, the style of Innocence in writing, is a way of getting out of something, it is a way of making things easy. And in the positive part of *Erewhon Revisited*, as in *News from Nowhere*, the intention is always that of making things easy. I have noted the strange abandonment of the difficulties of social converse in Morris's book. Mild high spirits and unexacting laughter are the substitute for more complicated attempts at social intercourse. And the same ghost haunts *Erewhon Revisited*; at the awkward moments there is always laughter and a kind of nursery jocularity to smooth things over. 'When we had laughed sufficiently over my mistake' (John Higgs to George, upon John's failure to keep their first appointment) is but one of a hundred references to a laughter that seems always at the command of these characters, though with the slimmest grounds for amusement. Again, one of the characters asked to be reminded to give an 'extra dose of kissing to Mrs Humdrum'. This is completely in the vein of Morris's Dick, to whom 'everything seems like a joke when we have a pleasant spell of work on, and good fellows merry about us'.

In the world-made-easy of the child's charade, the adult characters have no dignity; they are relieved of the necessity of dignity, and feel the easier for it. The adult being treated as a child—the theme which we have noticed in Lytton and in Butler—has clearly a fascination for both these writers.

CHAPTER VI

Samuel Butler and his Family Relations

This is an attractive book. Mrs Garnett's case is, of course, an unsatisfactory one. From time to time, in her rehabilitation of the characters of Butler's parents and sisters, she appears to suggest that because the cousins and acquaintances of the Butler household found Canon Butler a 'dear kindly humorous Uncle Butler, so full of pleasant jest and quip and kindliness', Butler, in his own picture of his father, must have misjudged him. This is clearly beside the point. Nothing in *The Way of All Flesh* suggests that Theobald might not appear a genial and kindly person to the outside world. And indeed it rather reinforces the general case of the book that the relations of son to father should be something so removed and concealed from the normal business of life that violent and uncivilized dramas could be enacted in the midst of a mild and gentle family existence. Again, the defence of sister May upon the grounds that she was universally liked, wrote pretty and facetious verses, and was eager to propitiate her brother, does not, as Mrs Garnett is herself evidently aware, provide any criticism of Butler's version of his sisters in the character of Charlotte. The lesson of the novel is, of course, that if the bringing-up of a child does go wrong, the most innocuous and amiable persons may for that child become instruments of an unendurable annoyance.

Mrs Garnett, in what she says in defence of the rest of the Butler household, says, except inadvertently, little that is relevant to Butler. This, of some blank verse of Harriet's, is a case in point:

...Of course it is no use offering *fondants* to those who do not like sweets; and I am sure that Samuel Butler would have seen in the poems I have given ample justification for his view! But I for one do not believe that superiority to 'prettiness' and the ordinary sentiments of ordinary people is entirely an advantage. One can be too superior. Does anyone seriously maintain that Butler was the greater for his dislike of Beethoven, Tennyson and Thackeray? *(F.R. 89)*

This confused defence of 'prettiness', 'the ordinary sentiments of ordinary people', and of 'Beethoven, Tennyson, and Thackeray', even if it were not in itself a little contradictory, would have no bearing upon Butler, and, indeed, defends what needed no defence. But Mrs Garnett can write more intelligently than this would suggest, and her own picture of Butler is, as far as it goes, persuasive.

The fact is that Butler was a man of extreme sensibility, and not a little lacking in moral robustness. . . . He could not face overt unpleasantness. . . . His attack was always sidelong, or even from behind. Of course this really needs as much courage (moral) as the other method. . . . But it does avoid the unpleasantness of the red face, the scowling eye, the blustering voice and the quick fist of the impulsive. . . . He had then no trace of the moral robustness that does not care a jot what is thought, which welcomes opposition, and is unmoved by vituperation. . . . He stabbed himself with every thrust at his enemies. *(F.R. 130)*

All this needed to be said, and is said decidedly well. Her final summing-up, for all its inadequacy, has also a certain ring of truth about it.

Consider well that passage I have quoted. . . . 'He felt bitter,—not because of anything his father had done to him,—but because he would never allow him to feel towards him as he was trying to feel.' His many and incessant efforts to reach an understanding, his long letters with their pages upon pages of explanation and defence—his offerings of plants and ferns—all tell the same story. When things went well, and father wrote amiable and friendly letters, he was happy. When they went ill, he was miserable; and he relieved himself by witty flippancies or profanities to Miss Savage. *(F.R. 223)*

96

But had it been more difficult to accept Mrs Garnett's view of Butler than it is, her book would still be valuable for the evidence which it provides. For it is here that we read for instance, of the incident of Harriet Butler's behaviour at the news of her brother's last illness. Butler was seriously ill at Naples, and his servant Alfred was sent out to bring him back to England. The yacht of one of Harriet's married nephews was lying off the coast, and could have been used for the journey, but Harriet 'dared not expose a young man to the contaminating influence of the infidel', and not till long afterwards did the nephew learn that he could have been of use. If one had any suspicions that the family ill-feeling had all been on Butler's side, and that to the end his family were only too ready to end the quarrel, this extraordinary act of Harriet's should put an end to them. Butler was evidently not alone in dramatizing the family relationships. One remembers the note (in *Further Extracts*) upon 'Wild Animals and one's Relations':

> If one would watch them and know what they are driving at, one must keep perfectly still.   (*F.E.* 112)

Harriet seems to have had the same feeling; she is on guard against her brother, as if indeed holding him off with a snake-handler's forked stick.

It is in Mrs Garnett's book, again, that we find the account of Festing Jones's behaviour at Butler's death-bed. May Butler's account of the conversation with Mr Jones is delightful:

> Mr Jones says that S. had a very real child-like practical belief in God. He often talked of God very simply and naturally....The question of immortality had ceased to interest him; not because he did not believe in it, but because it did not concern us now. It would be time enough to know about it then.

But he believed implicitly in an invisible world, and used to say that to deny it was the most unscientific and unreasonable thing in the world. 'It is not faith but simplest reason to believe in an invisible world. We know it' (not in any spiritualist sense, but because it answered to a part of our nature otherwise unexplained). Mr Jones says that he often spoke with the trust of a child.

(F.R. 144)

Mrs Garnett herself cannot quite swallow this as Butler's own expression of faith. And she jibs also at Jones's new-found piety, which so impresses May Butler.

I (May Butler writes) said it was not so much the great things in life, but the tiny ones which often made one feel how certainly there must be a God who knew and cared for us. I told him about my cold stopping your going; and Dr Lycett Burd being here when the telegram came; and Alfred's card coming just in time. He, Mr Jones, said he had felt exactly the same, that in many little ways he had been led and guided just right without his will in those last days. I am sure that if not in the fullest sense a believer in Christian truth (<i>he</i> sees no difficulty in miracle)—Mr Jones himself—is very close to it. (<i>F.R.</i> 145)

A niece of Butler's, in an account of a visit to Butler in his last illness, says, without making it perfectly clear whether she means Butler or Jones, 'He was horribly pathetic and was just going to cry, and we ran away.' After Jones's performance to May Butler one may have hopes that it was he who was horribly pathetic; though perhaps the venom of Malcolm Muggeridge's portrait of Jones is here leading one into unfairness.

CHAPTER VII

† Upon the Butler Collection at St John's College, Cambridge

IN that painstaking, competent and dead-looking study of the Interior of 15 Cliffords Inn, which is to be seen among the Butler paintings in the St John's collection, one detail, a tall black hat, dominates the whole scene. The hat stands upon a shelf in the angle of two walls; this shelf one imagines to have been built specially for the hat; and the hat itself seems to be sitting for its portrait. It is a pity if this hat has not found its way into the collections of Butler relics in the libraries of St John's, Cambridge, or Williams College, Massachusetts; for to that relic there would have attached a point which many other of those relics must be admitted to lack. It is a little ironical that it should be Butler to whose personal belongings posterity has given so reverential a care. I do not mean to say that it is surprising. The process of collection and of sanctification of these belongings had begun before Butler's death. Such a feeling for the value of posthumous fame as Butler possessed could not help but influence his own preparations for death. As we have seen, the rejection of possessions did not, for Butler, signify any lack of belief in the value of possession; it was merely the consequence of a desire to avoid any but personal possessions—prizes that were completely won or objects that were completely owned. The irony is in the fact that no one could have had duller possessions. Nothing strikes us so immediately about those crowded, barren, tidy, bachelor apartments of Butler's, which from photographs, descriptions and inventories we know so well, as the dullness which they represent.

One cannot but feel the pathos of those objects from which we are asked to remind ourselves of Butler, the tooth-brush and the kettleholder, the 'leather (or sham leather) cigarette case from Palermo', and the tobacco bowl that he delighted to tap and to make ring. Keats's books and papers have a note of tragedy in them, Byron's possessions have beauty and elegance, Burns's topboots and joint-stool are ridiculous enough to be pleasant; nobody takes such things seriously, because, though they may remind us of their owners, they tell us nothing about them. There is quite an industry of the faking of Burns's relics; every now and then a new public-house window, in Dumfriesshire, has a stanza scratched upon it, and an anecdote is invented in support of the inscription. It is a harmless enough industry, giving some pleasure and doing no damage. But of these pitiable and graceless remains of Butler, one's feeling must be different. Who would be at the trouble of faking a Butler relic? Who would profit by a spurious Butler toothbrush or find a buyer for another of his broken-down combs. The reputation is not strong enough to give value to *any* relic, and in consequence the poverty and dullness of these particular relics invades the observer's notions of the person they are intended to commemorate. One is bound to feel an indecency in the exhibition of these fusty personal objects, and the feeling extends to the manuscripts for which too much American money has been bid, and the bibliographies upon which too much care has been expended.

In the introduction to the catalogue, completed in 1945 by Carol A. Wilson, of the Butlerian possessions of the Chapin Library, Williams College, Williamstown, Massa-chusetts, it is left uncertain whether the predominant impulse behind the making of this collection was a respect for Butler or a desire to make a collection of *something*, and the discovery that Butler provided an easy subject. The tradition of Butler collections was already well established, the material was already in a good state of organization, and not over bulky; and as the writer remarks, it was felt to be a good thing for the reputation of Williams College to make a collection of this sort 'if for no other purpose, just to show students and others how such a collection should be made, and its scholastic value when it is made'. On the other hand, it is assumed that no one will question the fitness of building 'a United States Butler shrine', this being no more than a fitting tribute to 'a vital precursor of modern realism'.

It may seem of little moment whether we think an exact and comprehensive collection of Butler's writings of 'scholastic value' or not, or whether we think Butler deserves, or receives any advantage from, a shrine. But to me it does not seem an indifferent matter when one realizes the danger that the dullness and pointlessness of such pious accumulations may infect the whole reputation of their victim. The mixing of personal relics with published writings may easily lead to a confusion of values. For it is not as though the personal relics are such as might have belonged to any other famous Victorian. Their very dullness is characteristic of Butler, and has a meaning which may easily be overlooked. It was not a meaningless circumstance, as we have seen, that the main items of Butler's library were Bradshaw's Railway Guide and the Post Office Directory. And a meaning may equally be extracted from the tall hat that so dominated the rooms in Clifford's Inn. Worn, or merely exhibited on a shelf, the tall black hat was still the permanent symbol of normality. J. B. Yeats, in his *Recollections of Samuel Butler* has this interesting remark:

Butler was an Englishman through and through and an Englishman of 'class'. The Englishman of class will part with his faith, with his wife and children, with his money, even, or his reputation, and be cheerful about it, but closer than his skin sticks to him his class conceit, and in his accent, his voice, his gestures, his phrases, he carefully preserves all its insignia. (*Essays Irish & American*)

Whether or no the normality to which Butler adhered so tenaciously through all his literary outlawhood is best described as one of 'class', the fact that there was a normality with such a constant claim on him, is of importance. It is interesting to see in *A First Year in Canterbury Settlement* the young Butler painfully and obstinately adopting the 'normal' attitude of his new companions.

I have little to tell you concerning the Rangitata different from what I have already written about the Waimakiriri and the Harpur. The first great interest was of course finding the country which we took up; the next was what I confess to the weakness of having enjoyed much more—namely a most magnificent view of that most magnificent mountain, Mount Cook. (*F.Y.* 66)

and again

I am forgetting myself into admiring a mountain which is of no use for sheep. This is wrong. A mountain here is only beautiful if it has good grass on it. Scenery is not scenery—it is 'country', *subaudita voce* 'sheep'. If it is good for sheep, it is beautiful, magnificent, and all the rest of it; if not, it is not worth looking at. I am cultivating this tone of mind with considerable success, but you must pardon me for an occasional outbreak of the Old Adam. (*F.Y.* 71)

Later, when there was no longer the need for this particular normality, he could be sincere about the matter.

He liked to tell of his New Zealand life (says J. B. Yeats), and of his hatred of sheep. They were always getting lost, so that he said the word 'sheep' would be found engraved on his heart. He did not know one of his horses from another or from anybody else's horse, and said he was like the Lord, whose delight is not in the strength of a horse. (*Essays Irish & American*)

He was similarly ashamed at a later date of his acceptance at this time of a conventionally 'artistic' role, and was particularly contemptuous of the reference to Tennyson in *A First Year*:

> Under his bed I found Tennyson's *Idylls of the King*. So you will see that even in these out-of-the-world places people do care a little for something besides sheep.　　　　•　　　　(*F.Y.* 50)

The whole New Zealand episode is interesting in that it shows Butler's first reactions to the outside world and exhibits the beginnings of those tenacious orthodoxies within which he was to take refuge. The exclusive cult of Handel was evidently encouraged by those lonely evenings at the piano in the run 'at the back of beyond'. The rigid poses of the artist and the sheep-farmer must have reinforced each other; and whilst Butler's sudden intellectual release and access of power broke up the opinions of this period, a simultaneous social development was going on which gave the coltish-looking youth of the undergraduate photograph a protective set of whiskers, a repelling eye, a frigid manner, and a whole set of defensive orthodoxies.

It may be recalled that Butler justified his acceptance of the invitation to the Shrewsbury old boys' dinners on the grounds that he made himself sufficiently an outlaw by his writings and would only weaken his position by being also socially intransigeant. The slight touch of disproportion in this, the fact that Butler is here taking himself too seriously, is significant of his whole social attitude. In another age, one feels that Butler would have made a very successful eccentric. As an eccentric he would have been personally happier, and his influence as a man might easily have been strengthened. Eccentricity of life has never hurt good writing; and in Butler's case the constant social uneasiness and struggle, the painful devotion to normality, may be seen to have weakened and impeded his activity as a writer. The Victorian period did not lack its eccentrics, but it demanded the assurance of class and money for them. An eccentric would be an acceptable character only if he had the money or the position to make eccentricity his sole *métier*; there was still a place in society for a Hayley or a Beckford, but no longer one for a Nollekens. How often has one been surprised by the portraits of the Victorian period; there seems no connection between the queerness and idiosyncrasy of the talents of a Dodgson, a Clough and a Lear, and the solemn, normal faces that stare at the reader from the frontispieces of their books. They share with Gladstone and Darwin and the most accepted lions of the period the same steadfast public look of the elder statesman and *père de famille*. Nor is it merely a matter of clothes, and whiskers, and the professional photographer. Almost as much as the insufficiency of talent, it was the economic pressure of society which made the English aesthetic movement so signal a failure as compared with its French counterpart. Too many of its supporters found the economic necessity of a normal private life: Swinburne was tamed; Millais grew uncomfortable at his connection with the movement and abandoned both it and his best talent. One by one they were forced to make terms with society, or to go under altogether.

Butler on his return from New Zealand was tired out by a combat of another sort and had neither the conviction nor the toughness needed for a social combat. He had broken away from his parents, had made money, had exciting speculative ideas, and was going to paint. There was all the promise of a colourful career, but Butler was exhausted by the emergence from a disastrous childhood, he had clutched too desperately at social normality during his spiritual crisis; adventure, except of the intellectual kind, was no longer possible or attractive. Even at an unadventurous art class such as Heatherley's, it would have been difficult to be a less adventurous student of painting than Butler. J. B. Yeats tells the amusing and slightly pathetic story of Butler's endless, vain struggle to revive the style of Giovanni Bellini. Intellectually quite clear as to what his painting should be like, and at the same time conscious with one part of his mind of his own total lack of talent, Butler, from his seat nearest the model, pursued his minute and painstaking art with a desperate industry that years of irritation and failure could hardly impair.

He could not leave his outline until he had got it right, and there was a perpetual chase after the changing shadows. And when he had got the outline it was so constantly disappearing under the colour that he took to making 'a careful outline on a separate sheet of paper'; this was to be kept, after he had traced the drawing on to the paper which was to receive the colour, and to be referred to continually while he proceeded.   (*Recollections of Samuel Butler*)

Later, he adopted instead the camera obscura as a means of fixing outline, and for months was convinced he had found the key to painting. Always there was the assumption that industry alone, when applied along the best and most accepted lines, must produce, at some stage or other, a satisfactory result. It was the same with his music; Handel was the greatest of composers, therefore the determined study of conventional composition combined with a love of Handel must produce music worthy of Handel.

In his painting and his music, the delight, the adventure, the sense of pleasure that were the guide to his writing, deserted Butler. They became, like the Shrewsbury dinners, things that he knew he did not do well, but which publicly justified his existence. Not, indeed, that he thought of them in that way himself. Part of their meaning for him was that they represented his own hard-won independence.

It was the fruit of the stealing of his own birthright that he could amuse himself with whatever pursuit attracted him. But for all the reasonableness of this version, one can see that it was a false one. However clearly a situation might offer Butler the opportunity to amuse himself, to trifle gracefully, if there were also the opportunity to systematize, systematization won the day. Insulated so fully against the outside world, committed so fully to a regularized, fenced-in, self-reflecting bachelor existence, an existence in which routine prolonged plans, the original stimulus to which might long ago have lost its force, Butler was prevented from employing his own pleasure-test (the method 'Of knowing what one likes') in the very cases where it was most required. The theory of the test-by-pleasure made it evident that painting and composition were the *kind* of thing that he enjoyed, but for want of commerce with the outside world, Butler was prevented from applying the test day by day to the detail of these occupations. The pain which the prolonged experiment in painting caused Butler is evinced by a dozen references in his Letters and Note-books; the pleasure is never made evident. All through that period, the cultivation of an admirable prose shows the presence of the strongest faculty for enjoyment; the saving and blessed unprofessionality of literature kept alive the dilettante that painting was to have gratified and in fact only stifled. The painting and the composition, and perhaps, too, the Homeric studies, from which the pleasure seems to have evaporated long before the systematizing impetus was exhausted, should to my mind be thought to belong to the world of the tall black hat, the closed, conventional, unsatisfying world of protective normality.

One could express the division which I have noted in Butler's attitude to life as a conflict between the dilettante and the pedagogue. For all the dissipation of energy which Butler's work exhibits, it still everywhere shows traces of the desire to exercise authority. However small the point to which he gives attention—the assignment of a picture or a chapel-figure to its correct author or subject—Butler never for a moment doubts the value of an authoritative view of the matter.

But the assumption of *authority* is the clue to another side of Butler, and in particular to the nature of his influence. The title of a popular Edwardian book, *Prophets, Priests and Kings* by A. G. Gardiner, throws an interesting light upon the Edwardian period. In this period, to which the growth of Butler's present reputation belongs, the name 'prophet' came to have a new and important significance. In the English literary world, the characteristic figures—Shaw, Wells, Chesterton and so on—did not perhaps gain a completer possession of the minds of the average intelligent young man than the spectacular figures of earlier periods; but the possession that they gained was of a different kind. The suggestion of the Edwardian 'prophet' was, more explicitly and persuasively than one sees it in earlier literary messiahs, that of 'Be like me'. The intelligent young man could *be* a Shaw or a Wells to himself in a way that he could not have *been* to himself a Byron or a Carlyle. Shaw, and it is in this that his indebtedness to Butler is most evident, makes frequent and explicit demands for discipleship. The device by which personal imitation is made possible and attractive is the use of the notion of *courage*. When Shaw or Wells are making their most direct appeal to discipleship, they will usually be found to be presenting a proposition of this sort: 'You see how much intellectual lumber a man can get rid of and be none the worse for it; have the courage to do the same, and you will be like me.'

With Chesterton the proposition was necessarily different; but it involved equally the notion of courage. The swash-buckling, gallant, paradoxical style, the bravado and intellectual high-spirits, were directed to conveying a right personality; the suggestion is 'See how happy a person a brave attitude to life has made me; have the same courage, and you will be the same.' This type of prophetizing is always concerned with the advertisement of a personality. It is the difference between a local phenomenon such as Shaw and a European one such as Voltaire that Shaw is, as it were, acting the part of a Voltaire. The hint given by Ibsen's self-dramatization leads to the constant and finally self-destructive posturing of Shavian dialogue. We know the hero of *The Enemy of the People* to be Ibsen; but in a play of Shaw's there will be a dozen Shaws scoring characteristic victories over as many lay-figures. In the midst of an admirably sharp, amusing, athletic dialogue, there are moments of the personal *grab*; the emotional design upon the observer is as naked as that of the melo-drama which is being burlesqued; at a dozen moments there is the direction 'Be like this'.

A quotation from Butler's Notebooks, of which I have already made use, may be repeated here:

> There is no conception of the faith that a man should do his duty cheerfully with all his might though, as far as he can see, he will never be paid directly or indirectly either here or hereafter. Still less is there any conception that unless a man has this faith he is not worth thinking about. There is no sense that as we have received freely so we should give freely and be only too thankful that we have anything to give at all.... (*NB.* 189)

Butler, in speaking of Bunyan, makes the remark which Shaw, and many since Shaw, have made upon the subject of Pascal. That argument which Pascal frequently uses to recommend faith, viz. that, if nothing else, faith is a good investment, that it is at least an intelligent speculation, as much as backing the favourite in a horse-race, when one has no better criterion to go by than that of the bookmaker's odds, was one most calculated to offend the Shavian disciple. The objection levelled against it was that it was cowardly; and cowardice in intellectual matters had for the true Edwardian intellectual become the final condemnation. A nervous and spectre-haunted generation such as the present must be a little amazed at the confidence in the virtues of intellectual courage which the Edwardian displayed. The flight into the Catholic church of the nineteen-twenties and nineteen-thirties was a radically different affair from the *fin-de-siècle* or the Chesterton-Belloc movements in the same direction; the stimulus of both the latter was some kind of courage; at their period it was still original and socially adventurous to be a Catholic convert. In the 'twenties and 'thirties the courageous attitude had exhausted its attractions; no one now believed in the virtues of any manipulation of attitude; the search was on for the refuge beyond all attitudes, the concealed paradise, the life beneath or beyond the personality.

That Shaw derived his 'brave' attitude from Butler would overstate the case. The attitude is expressed most fully in the work published after Butler's death. And even the clearest statement of it, the one which I have quoted, has its partial disclaimer:

> Furthermore there does not appear to be even the remotest conception that this honourable, comfortable and sustaining faith is, like all other high faiths, to be brushed aside very peremptorily at the bidding of common-sense. (*NB*. 189)

None the less, examining one's earliest and most abiding impression of Butler, one sees that it is that of an

Edwardian prophet. The anecdotes, the attack upon family life in *The Way of All Flesh*, the familiar aphorisms, all fill out the picture of the brave and cheerful nihilist upon the Shavian pattern. The mischievousness, the 'wickedness' which lose their force as one penetrates into the details of the life and work, make up almost the whole of that original impression.

We are such an inveterately idolatrous people that it would perhaps be well for us if we could go back frankly to the cultus of the graven image, and leave our great men unworshipped. It would take the conceit out of them and do the graven images no harm.... We are overburdened with gods and sects; our Walhalla is as disorderly as the Church of the Holy Sepulchre, in which Moslem soldiers keep the Christian worshippers from coming to blows with one another, would be without the soldiers. We are Gladstonians, Wagnerians, Pasteurians, Burne-Jonesians, Browningites, Marxites, Darwinians, or else we belong to the simply heathen majority.

So wrote Shaw in the *Pall Mall Gazette* of 1887 in a review of Butler's *Luck or Cunning?* The language could almost be Butler's own, and the matter has its relevance to my present point. The idolatry of the Wagnerite and the Darwinian was not the idolatry of the Edwardian disciple, but perhaps the one led to the other. It was not for nothing that Shaw's own vegetarianism became so familiar a public fact. And can we not see in the popularity of Festing Jones's *Life of Butler* a further stage of the same idolatry? To read of the most minor details of a man's life, to examine his reactions to the most trivial and indifferent situations, must have an acute interest for the thorough-going disciple. In such details he can see how the trick was done. Reading with the perennial question in his mind, 'Can I be like this?', the disciple cannot feel indifferent towards even the most minor circumstance. No doubt the vices of our contemporary biography and autobiography may be partly accounted for in this way. The mountain of anecdotal and personal detail, which the modern biography presents, detail not interesting as representative of a society or of a period of history, not ordered with any judicial purpose, lacking all other function than that of the snapshot, cannot but correspond to an appetite in the reading public. Most modern biography aspires to the condition of the Life of a Royal person. Detail hardly less fatuous than that which fills out the court circular of the daily newspaper provides the material of many lengthy biographies and autobiographies of the day. Interest in character (the Boswellian interest) gives way to interest in personality, and in something even more arbitrary than personality. Of this sort of interest Festing Jones's *Life of Butler* is a notable expression. It is the interest, dignified by the formality of literary externals, of the souvenir and the autograph-album. And one may point to the Edwardian brand of idolatry as at least a partial cause of this fashion. Once the charm is broken, once the personality has ceased in general to attract, the detail becomes as expressionless and dead as the anonymous souvenir. The boredom of the traditional hagiography will be nothing to that which will be possessed after a few years by those Lives written by A Friend which week by week our Sunday newspapers recommend to us.

If at a long remove of time some future commentator were unlucky enough to confuse or to amalgamate two late Victorians, Samuel Butler and Oscar Wilde, the facts would provide at least a Baconian justification. Single authorship would account very conveniently for the quotations from memory and reversed proverbs to which both Butler and Wilde were addicted; further, both wrote studies of Shakespeare's sonnets and came to similar conclusions; both, again, wrote celebrated works the point of which rested to no small degree on a pun upon the name of Ernest. 'Why should An Earnest (I hate the word) Clergyman do so?' wrote Butler in a letter to the *Examiner* in 1879; and from that we may gauge the degree of self-hatred which led to the creation of Ernest Pontifex. And after all, would the confusion be altogether meaningless? I have the feeling that at no very remote period the radical opposition between the two writers will be less obvious than their connection.

In Wilde and Butler an intimate personal grievance against society led to rather similar results; for different reasons both were liable to think of themselves in the role of outlaw; Butler's devastating family conflict and Wilde's perversion had the effect of giving a personal complexion to their quarrel with society. The quarrel becomes a family affair; a constant skirmishing warfare with society, conducted in that genre of epigram which depends upon the frustration of stock response, came to have the air of a permanent marital tiff. With Wilde, of course, there was the piratical excitement; for him there was the adventure of imposing himself upon the society which he despised. To upset and to charm were for Wilde two rules of the same game. The opposition to Butler's attitude is in this point complete. For Butler the essential was to avoid all *personal* dealings with the society with which as a writer he had so constant a quarrel. To avoid the pain and damage that society could inflict was a cardinal object of Butler's policy. Wilde's tragedy, indeed, should be seen as the counterpart of Butler's exaggerated prudence. The perils of normality and the perils of eccentricity could not be better demonstrated than by the personal histories of these two writers. The dullness and dowdiness of Butler's plan for living, the graceless apartments and the dreary possessions, may be thought of as the logical alternative to the perilous life of determined eccentricity. Wilde as he was photographed upon landing in America, in the full splendour of his 'impeccable bad taste', opulent, florid, and successful, in Florentine cloak and luxuriant cravat, with beringed fingers and painted face—how exactly and neatly he contrasts with the Butler of a dozen pictures, a clumsy comfortable figure in baggy trousers and shapeless coat, a beard taking all expression from the mouth, and in the eyes, to which pince-nez give an illusion of primness, a look at once defiant and uneasy. Tragedy hovers unmistakably over the photograph of Wilde; the grotesque abandon of his appearance suggests the irresistibility of the social forces pushing him towards disaster. There is a tragic exaggeration in the whole display, a superhuman enlargement which denotes the tragic victim. In the pictures of Butler, with which we confront the more than life-size image of the doomed Wilde, each detail aids the effect of intentional and protective dullness. A concealed life, a resolute refusal of tragedy by a character naturally inclining to it: such, perhaps, in that age, and for that temperament, was the one available alternative to the fatal choice of Wilde.